1989

Te

)

0

7

GW00480686

MULLYON

ITS HISTORY, SCENERY AND ANTIQUITIES

A facsimile of the edition first published in 1875

E G HARVEY B.A.

DYLLANSOW TRURAN

This facsimile edition of the original published by
Dyllansow Truran
Cornish Publications
Trewolsta, Trewirgie, Redruth, Cornwall

First published 1875

This edition first published 1984

Printed and bound in Great Britain by A. Wheaton & Co. Ltd, Exeter

ISBN 0 907566-70-7

CAVE AT PORTHPYG, MULLYON COVE

From a water-colour painting by Rev. F. C. Jackson, now in possession of Walter J. Goldsmith, Esq.

MULLYON:

ITS HISTORY, SCENERY AND ANTIQUITIES;

NARRATIVES OF SHIPWRECKS ON ITS COAST;

ITS AGRICULTURE, FISHERIES, AND MINING;

TALES OF THE DAYS OF WRECKING AND SMUGGLING;

LONGEVITY OF ITS INHABITANTS;

NAMES OF PLACES, THEIR TRUE CORNISH RENDERINGS AND SIGNIFICATIONS,

&c., &c., &c.

Predannack Cross, page 18.

"Remember that whilst we are searching for the history of by-gone days the scenes before our eyes vanish and are forgotten. Stereotype then, as it were, the present, and afterwards trace back to the earliest times."

Cornwall Register.

BY

E. G. HARVEY, B.A., VICAR.

TRURO:

W. LAKE, PRINCES STREET.

LONDON:

SIMPKIN, MARSHALL, & Co., STATIONERS' HALL COURT.

1875.

TO THE RIGHT HONOURABLE

LORD ROBARTES,

WHOSE READY SYMPATHY AND GENEROUS AID

HAVE EVER BEEN EXTENDED

TO ALL GOOD WORKS IN THE PARISH OF MULLYON,

THE FOLLOWING PAGES

ARE, WITH PERMISSION, RESPECTFULLY INSCRIBED

BY

THE AUTHOR.

TABLE OF CONTENTS.

LIST OF ILLUSTRATIONS.

———

ERRATA ET CORRIGENDA.

Page   3.—Eleventh line from bottom, for "is" read "are."

  „   39.—Second line from bottom, "the curving valley" (quasi 'guris.')
This etymology is doubtful, see page 109.

  „   62.—Second line, for "Mansbury's" read "Manby's."

  „   96.—Eighth line from bottom, for "daw" read "dau, dou."

  „   97.—Seventh line from bottom, for "dew gain" read "deugain."

  „   97.—Second line from bottom, for "19 by 15 + 4" read "18 by 15 + 3;"
and strike out "18" at end of the line.

  „   98.—Fifteenth line from bottom, for "cyfodd" read "cyfododd."

  „   98.—Sixth line from bottom, for "San" read "Lan."

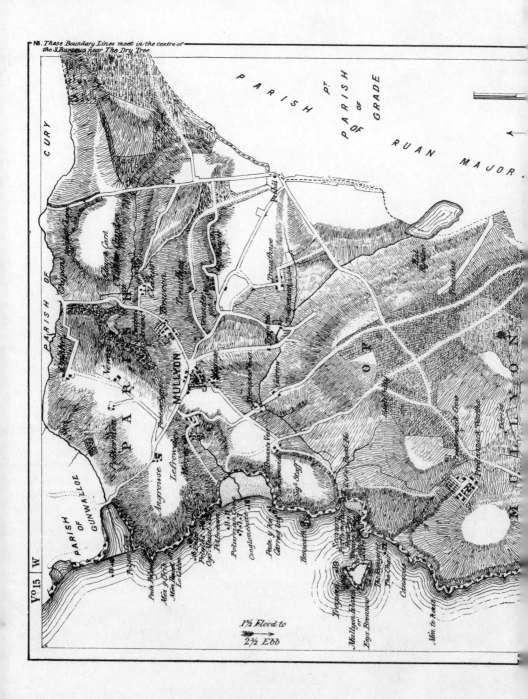

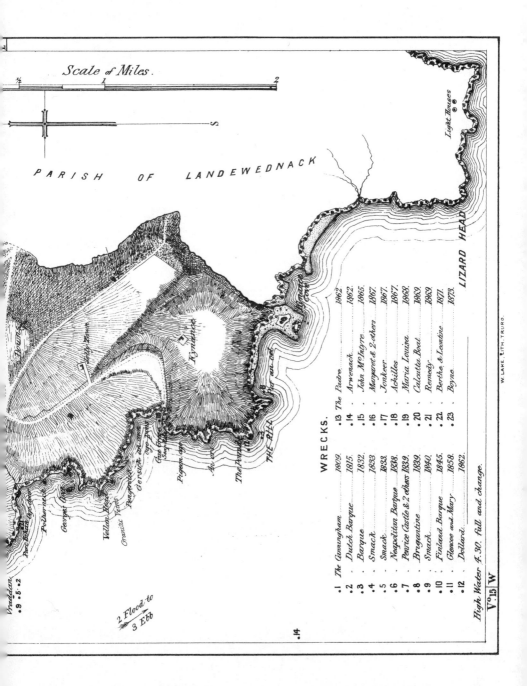

Scale of Miles.

PARISH OF LANDEWEDNACK

LIZARD HEAD

Light Houses

WRECKS.

High Water. F. 30. full and change.

1	The Cunningham	1809.	13	The Padre	1862.
2	Dutch Barque	1815.	14	Arwenack	1862.
3	Barque	1832.	15	John M⁰hayre	1865.
4	Smack	1833.	16	Margaret & 2 others	1867.
5	Smack	1833.	17	Jonkeer	1867.
6	Neapolitan Barque	1838.	18	Achilles	1867.
7	Pewrice Castle & 2 others	1839.	19	Maria Louisa	1868.
8	Brigantine	1839.	20	Calcutta Brvl.	1869.
9	Smack	1840.	21	Remedy	1869.
10	Finland Barque	1845.	22	Berthe, & Leontine	1871.
11	Glencoe and Mary	1858.	23	Boyne	1873.
12	Dollard	1862.			

V⁰15 W

2 Flood to
3 Ebb

W. LAKE. LITH. TRURO.

MULLYON.

THE Parish of Mullyon, lying in Meneâg, in the Archdeaconry of Cornwall, and in the Deanery and Hundred of Kirrier, is bounded on the North by Cury and Gunwalloe, on the East by Ruan Major and Grade, on the South by Landewednack, and on the West by the Sea. It covers 4,786 acres of land, of which 1,700 are arable, 1,200 pasture, and the rest commons, crofts, and public roads.

The gross estimated rental is £3,475, the rateable value £3,086; and the population, by the the census of 1871, numbered 695.

The tithes are commuted at £535, of which £225 are vicarial, and £310 impropriated.

The patronage of the living is in the Bishop of Exeter.

In the valuation of Pope Nicholas, which was made during the reign of Edward the First, in the years 1288 to 1291, appears the following:

TAXACIO DE ECCLĪAR' ARCHID' CORNUB'
Decanatus de Kere (Kirrier).

	Taxacio.	*Decim.*
Ecclĩā Scī Mellani	£8 0 0	8 4

In the *Valor Ecclesiasticus, temp. Henry VIII.*, it is entered as Melyan, and in legal documents, *temp. Elizabeth*, as Mullyan.

S. Mellion, in the East of Cornwall, is also spoken of as S. Mellanus.

The name is variously given in our parish register as St. Mullyon, Mullyon, S. Mullian, Mullian, Mullyan, Mulion, St. Mullion, and Mullion. In the registry, at Exeter, it is now given as Mullyon ; hence I, as " Vicar of Mullyon," have adopted this form.

S. Mellonus is called S. Malo by Usher ; and Dr. Oliver decides that Mellonus, Malo and Meen are identical, and seeing that we have S. Malo's Moor in the parish to this day, I would rather suppose that S. Malo, a Briton by birth, gave the name to this parish, than go out of my way to seek, as some have done, in the Persian language, for a word resembling ' Mullyon,' and meaning ' smooth,'—particularly as there is nothing smooth about us either by sea or on land—than trace it to the plant ' Mullen,' which really grows in much greater abundance in the surrounding parishes than with us, or, than place myself under the patronage of St. Melanie or Melina, an obscure saint in the Roman calendar, who lived principally in Rome, Carthage, and Jerusalem, and who never, as far as is known, attempted a visit to these shores.

But more of this by-and-bye, when I come to speak of the church and its dedication.

Excepting what is ecclesiastical, the history of Mullyon is somewhat scanty. There is evidence of the Manor of Predannack being held by the family of Serjeaux.* Richard, of that ilk, M.P. for the county of Cornwall, in the time of Richard the Second, possessed it, and he dying without issue, it fell to his sisters as co-heiresses. The youngest of the three carried it in marriage to Vere, Earl of Oxford. Sir Richard Robartes was seized of the manor of Predannack Wartha, and Predannack Wollas, in the 17th James the First, 1619. Part of the latter now belongs to Sir R. R. Vyvyan, Bart., but the rest of the manor is the property of Lord Robartes. From the Calendars of Proceedings in Chancery, in the reign of Queen Elizabeth we abstract the following : " John Hodge, *alias* Richards, plaintiff, Robert Richards and Stephen John, defendants, concerning a tenement called Trenant (Trenance), in the parish of Mullyan, the inheritance of Richard Boscawen, and by him devised to Richard Hodge *alias* Richards, plaintiff's father." Vol. 11, p. 45. H.h. 16.

* See appendix A.

Trenance is now in the possession of Lord Robartes.

Again, " Michael Tresagher, *alias* Tresaugher, generosus, and Anna, his wife, sold lands in Vounder, Trewoone, and the Church Town of Mullyon, all in this parish, to William Peres, *alias* Pryske." 25 Eliz., 1582.

Vounder now belongs to Viscount Falmouth. Indeed, Lord Robartes and Viscount Falmouth are the principal land owners of the parish, smaller portions belonging respectively to Sir R. R. Vyvyan, C. H. Hawkins, Esq., Messrs. J. B. Kempthorne, and Peter Williams.

As regards the soil the greater part of the parish rests on a bed of serpentine, and strangers are wont to form large ideas of the vastness of our riches when we tell them that we not only build our houses, but even pave our roads with serpentine, but northward of a line drawn from the centre of Polurrian Cove to Clahar Garden, the slate formation presents itself, which may be traced northward along the coast till it meets the granite spur of Tregoning Hill, at Trewavas Cliffs. There are two patches of hornblende, also, one extending from Polurrian Cove, near which are traces of ochre and iron-stone, to Porthmellin and the stream that runs into it, being separated from the slate at the former place by a well marked vein of conglomerate, and extending inland to the neighbourhood of Church Town. Another mass of hornblende will be found between Predannack and the sea. Then there is the Soap Rock (so called from its being unctuous to the touch) in the valley of Gue Greze traversing the serpentine in large veins. Particulars of the raising of this peculiar formation is given below.

"Native," or pure malleable copper has from time to time been found in large lumps or veins in the interstices of the serpentinic rock, mostly in the valley just north of Predannack Wartha where mining was once carried on at a great cost. One mass of native copper was sent from this to the Exhibition of 1851, weighing 15 cwt. " The metal bore the appearance of having been poured in a melted state into the crevices of the rocks, it was for the most part flattened, and branched at the edges ; it had the lustre of a new copper coin, and had here and there adhering to its side portions of steatite of a beautiful grass green." The cost of boring the solid serpentine was not however defrayed by the occasional " find " of a beautiful branched and glistening tree of bright and lustrous copper, and the mining operations were necessarily given up.

The principal crops raised in Mullyon are wheat, barley, oats, turnips and mangolds. These last do so remarkably well that it is almost a wonder that some speculative genius is not tempted to grow beet for the sugar manufacture. As in West Cornwall generally all kinds of vegetables are early, while the harvests are late and " catchy."

The lobster and crab fisheries in the spring, and the pilchard seine fishery in the autumn, give employment to a large number of the inhabitants.

RAMBLES THROUGH THE PARISH.

RAMBLE NO. I.

MULLYON, within its comparatively small area, presents almost every variety of scenery that may be found within these latitudes. From the bare uncultivated heath whose silence is only broken by the distant murmur of the sea, you may descend by short and easy steps to the deep and thickly wooded dell, whose sombre recesses are enlivened by the perpetual babbling of its noisy brook. From the placid quiet of the homestead and well cultivated farm you may pass at once out upon the imposing grandeur of the high beetling cliff, whose weather beaten tops and cragged sides tell tales of anything but peaceful elements; and a meditative ramble along the productive *cwms* may be varied within a very short distance by an equally interesting stroll on one of the many sandy beaches of our brine-washed coves.

Are you for a tramp, good reader, across the breezy *gûns*—
"Oh, who will o'er the downs with me."

Then come along, let us start from the Vicarage; but first let me put a biscuit or two in my pocket, my little flask of schnaps, and my pocket compass. "Why the last?" do you say. Well, it may not be necessary, but I've lost myself before now in a sudden fog on the downs when I should have been glad to have had it with me. But come along, down through the meadows to the southward along the now nearly obliterated church path,* across the

---

* This unfortunately is not the only church path in the parish that is being gradually lost sight of. The direct path across the valley to Cury by Newton and Gwills is fast disappearing. The church path to La Floudre and that through Park Venton, and Gweal an Drea, in Tremenhehe, though one of the best and most frequented in the parish, is not marked in the parish map. The present generation do not think the appoint-

stream, and up through Garrow farm—the rough *(arrow)* bit of land—is it not rightly named? and so out upon the down. Flat is it not, this high table land? Not much depth of soil? No; they have a suicidal plan here of scarifying the surface to that extent that there is not much chance of any soil collecting; the moment any does make its appearance it is carefully shaved off with a shovel to burn on their open hearths.

The true Cornish heath, *erica vagans*, is not so plentiful here as in some other parts of the downs; but the pretty waxen little *tetralix* is common enough. That large pool away to the left is Hâl Kymbro—the Britons—but why so called I can't say. It is not often you get a winter here sufficiently severe for the ice to bear; yet, in February, 1870, I had the pleasure of a good run on the pattens to the wonder and amaze of the villagers who had never seen a pair of skates before. That church tower right a-head, with only three pinnacles, is S. Ruan Major; its fourth pinnacle was injured during a thunder storm, on the 7th Sunday after Trinity, 26th July, 1868. Mullyon church was struck by lightning during the same storm and part of the parapet of its tower sent whizzing down through the roof. The electric fluid also entered at the west end, and running up the northern row of arches, made its exit at the east window, knocking off a portion of one of the pillars, and covering the chancel with bits of stone and plaster. This happily occurred between the services, when the church was empty. But S. Ruan's pinnacle was rendered so unsafe that the parishioners, to avoid accidents, thrust its remains bodily over—a much simpler course, you will say, than restoring the pinnacle. They seem to be of your opinion. But here we are at Hervan Gutter. Here it was that the ghost of Thomas Flavel, former vicar of Mullyon and rector of Ruan, himself a famous exorcist, was laid by a brother cleric, of whom Flavel had said, " When he comes I must go." And here, at the entrance to the lane, on the right, are the remains of a tumulus which was opened under the direction of W. C. Borlase, Esq., on 11th November, 1871. We were present at the opening, and have preserved parts of an earthen urn,

---

ment of Churchwardens— whose duty it is among other things to look-after the church paths—necessary. Whether the children will by-and-bye be of the same opinion, or will thank their forefathers for neglecting their interests, is dubious. The roadway from La Floudre to Trenance Vean, which once formed part of the old road to the Lizard, has only lately been blocked.

of very rough manufacture, which contained relics of calcined bones and charcoal.

But let us away again over the downs to Jolly Town—a jovial place indeed! Can you imagine anything more dreary or desolate? Look every way, can you see even a shrub? Here is an attempt at grass to be sure, but whatever could have induced the first settler to fix on such a spot? There is positively no road by which to approach the cot, and in winter the down all round you is ankle deep in mud and water. It is a nice airy situation indeed, and if you are fond of solitude this is the spot for you, just the place of which you might predicate that it was about "five miles from anywhere." We might now run down that valley to Gue Greze, and the Soap rock, but we will leave that for another day, and pass on to Predannack Head.

What a glorious prospect! The rocky Vellan headland to your left, and in front of you the whole stretch of Mount's Bay—Tol Pedn, or Old Land's End, reaching far out into the horizon, S. Buryan church tower (Castle Treryn and Lamorna Cove are easily distinguishable with a glass), Chapel Carn Bre (640 feet), not looking as if it really were 20 miles off, Newlyn, Penzance, in the extreme hollow of the bay, the sands of Eastern Green backed by Castle-an-Dinas (735 feet), the Mount—*the* Mount, of course, for there is no other Mount to a Cornishman—the rugged rocks of Cuddan, the granite cliffs at Trewavas, Tregoning Hill (596 feet), the three mile stretch of sandy beach from Porthleven to Pedngwinnion, and then that glorious reach of alternate lofty cliff and sandy cove terminating with the Gull Rock, and with Mullyon Island almost at your feet. There are few, if any, pictures, even in the romantic district of Meneag to equal this.

When your eye has satisfied itself we'll saunter on along the edge of the cliff to Mullyon Cove or Porthmellin. But think, as you gaze upon this now placid scene, what miserable shipwrecks have occurred, what numerous lives have been lost on this, by nature, inhospitable coast, before and beneath you. And again, what contraband cargoes have been run, and, for all we know, what desperate encounters have taken place on these solemn, silent, awe-inspiring rocks. That perpendicular bluff at Mên-y-Grib, about two miles off, witnessed, in the dead of night, the instantaneous perishing of four and twenty precious souls.

Nearer, that old grey mass that lifts its lofty head in pinnacles between Polurrian and Henscath, saw fifteen more swept to destruction, not leaving one to tell the tale how or why they came there. Here below is Canavas, and the Chair, the Rinyard and Vro sand, where, before now, hundreds, perhaps thousands, of kegs, that never saw the customs, have been landed. But proceed. Mullyon Island—Enys Pruen, as it was formerly called, has oft been likened to a huge beast reclining in the sea. For myself, it requires a stretch of imagination to discover the similarity; but, if there be at all a likeness, it is to be seen from hence. And here is the Gull rock, with its sheer seaward face, Do you note how the gulls and the puffins and the cormorants hold each their appropriated portions of the rock? Well! that matter was only definitely settled about five years ago, and then only after a dreadful war of twelve hours' duration, the din of which reached even to Church Town. How long the present pacific arrangements shall last—*quien sabe?* Now, over this bit of down and then descend into the Cove. Here is the house which contains our lifeboat—a noble boat she is, and the largest on our Cornish coast; but I will tell you more about her by and bye. Here lie our seine boats, and there, the crabbers'; but come down to this narrow cleft in the hill, and through the natural tunnel out on the sands of Porth Pyg. "Mullyon Cove," says the late Dean Alford in the November number, 1868, of *Good Words* (which also contains several pretty little sketches by the lamented Dean), "Mullyon Cove is vast in extent and unites in itself, in its various parts, almost all the characteristics of Cornish coast scenery. It is rather an assemblage of subjects than a subject in itself. . . By threading a curious chink in a rock to the South you open upon a lovely beach of yellow sand, with any amount of variously grouped rocks for a foreground, and, if you please, a noble cave to arch your picture." But that is not the cave we shall visit presently. It is just now three-quarter ebb spring tide, and we could not have a better opportunity for penetrating this much neglected *ogo*. Comparisons are often made between Mullyon Cove and Kynance— "comparisons are odious"—but they are not to be compared, they are in their formation and character so very different. I should say that where Kynance is pretty, Mullyon Cove is grand; but we will be content to admire both, each in its several characteristics, and without prejudice or jealousy, for we can but remember that all the beauties of Kynance also lie in the parish of Mullyon. Do you know Italy? Have you seen the slopes of Vesuvius? Does this black brown mass of serpentinic formation at all remind you of a layer of lava? A Cornishman would say it was not unlike "slag" from the smelting house cooled down, and cracked in all directions in the cooling. But here is the entrance to the cave, and here is the old fisher-man, Sam Hitchens, with his bundle of furze and tar-dipped torch to lighten up its innermost recesses. As you go in, notice that bit of timber high above your head, and jammed so tightly between the rocks. That is a portion of the barque Chinchas that became a total wreck on the Loe Bar, in 1859. It was washed over here, and has been firmly held there ever since. This cave, or *ogo*, says Mr. Johns, "is a striking object when seen externally, yet the view from within is yet more so—impenetrable gloom above—brilliant light streaming in through the fissures, but revealing nothing behind—the smoothest of all possible sands—little pools of water, so still that not even a sunbeam is seen to dance on them—richly dark walls, so polished as to reflect the light with a splendour scarcely to be endured—the blue sea, with its curled edging of snow-white lace—St. Michael's Mount, the fabled 'tower in the sea,' in the distance." But Sam is lighting up; let us go in. Eh! what does he look like behind the smoke, and the flames flickering and dancing about him and on the polished sides of this huge cleft? This must be seen to be appreciated. No description could convey its weirdness to the imagination. Stay now, and admire it as you please, but take care that you are not caught by the returning tide.

CHARACTER, RELIGION, &c.

———

WE have not many records, of the character of the earlier inhabitants of Mullyon, yet of the date, particularly in Cornwall, when

"Saints were many and sins were few,"

we may, in some measure, judge by the relics that have come down to us. They, the men of those times, were probably of that independent spirit and uncertain temperament so often now observable in Cornishmen—hospitable and affable, volatile and capricious, unstable, yet sympathetic ; sometimes, nevertheless, possessing the curt, treacherous qualities of your true Celt.

As to the character of the present inhabitants, it will hardly become me to say anything here further than what would be on all hands allowed, that one would not expect to find among the dwellers in a parish which is wholly agricultural, the mental capacity or quickness of intellect observable in the occupiers of a mining district, while a greater amount of cautious, yet timid reticence, may easily be detected.

I cannot, however, refrain from saying, that during a residence of ten years among a people, who, from whatever cause, simply hate the Church, and who look upon the Parson as a sort of Ecclesiastical Policeman, I have personally met with respectful civility and attention, particularly from the labourers and fishermen ; the exceptions have been where simple ignorance of their own ignorance, or the virulence of an unreasoning prejudice has led others astray to unbecoming words and actions.

Of the religious persuasions I may be permitted to state, as facts, that the majority of the present parishioners affect that form which is known as "The United Methodist Free ;" and there are also a large number of "Wesleyan

Methodists," each of these bodies having commodious preaching houses of their own. The number of Churchmen is few. No fault of theirs, indeed ; and I would hope none of mine. But this is not remarkable when, within the memory of those living in the parish now, there was but one Curate, and not one resident Incumbent, in charge of three parishes. Then there are also a few " good home Christians," as they call themselves, who never go to any place of worship.

Baptisms are administered indiscriminately in the church, at the preaching houses, and in private. Marriages are performed in the parish church, and before the Registrar, in Helston ; and there is but one burial-ground—the Church-yard—for all.

But to return to the former subject—the character and general bearing of the inhabitants. I will quote the works of two celebrated men, one of whom wrote in the year 1817, the other in 1872 ; and when I mention the fact that both are ministers of the Anabaptist persuasion, a religious denomination that is not represented in Mullyon, though, therefore, as might be supposed, viewing matters through the same medium, it will be admitted that their judgment will be unbiassed, and their conclusions independent and possibly without prejudice. My first authority is the Rev. G. C. Smith, of Penzance, formerly an officer in the Royal Navy (British Boatswain), and I quote from a work of his, published in 1817, entitled, " The Wreckers, or a Tour of Benevolence from S. Michael's Mount to the Lizard Point." He speaks particularly of the village of Predannack.

" Our friends, in H———, have lately begun preaching here, but they
" want help ; this is a most excellent station for an itinerant ; it lies in the
" parish of Mullyon, about four miles from the Lizard. There is no preach-
" ing whatever in this village, and there are some who cannot walk far out
" of it. The neighbourhood is sadly infested with the wreckers. When
" the news of a wreck flies round the coast, thousands of people are
" instantly collected near the fatal spot ; pick-axes, hatchets, crow-bars, and
" ropes, are their usual implements for breaking up and and carrying off what-
" ever they can. The moment the vessel touches the shore she is considered
" fair plunder, and men, women, and children are working on her to break

" her up, night and day. The precipices they descend, the rocks they climb,
" and the billows they buffet, to seize the floating fragments, are the most
" frightful and alarming I ever beheld ; the hardships they endure (especially
" the women) in winter to save all they can, are almost incredible.   Should a
" vessel, laden with wine or spirits, approach the shore, she brings certain
" death and ruin, to many, with her.   The rage and fighting to stave in
" the casks and bear away the spoil, in kettles and all manner of vessels, is
" brutal and shocking.   To drunkenness and fighting, succeed fatigue, sleep,
" cold, wet, suffocation, death, and—what ? an eternity !   Last winter we had
" some dreadful scenes of this description.   A few in this neighbourhood, it
" seems, having a little more light than others, scrupled to visit a wreck that
" came on shore last winter, on a Lord's day, lest it should be breaking the
" Sabbath ; but they gathered all their implements into a public house, and
" waited until the clock struck twelve—at midnight, therefore. they rushed
" forth, all checks of conscience being removed.   Imagine to yourself, 500
" little children in a parish, brought up every winter in this way, and en-
" couraged, both by precept and example, to pursue this horrid system."

Now, I imagine that some of the above should be taken *cum grano salis ;*
as, for instance, 500 is a large number of children to allot to a parish whose
total population is not known to have exceeded 800 ; but then it should also
be remembered that he wrote from what he saw.   My next authority had not
that advantage.   The Rev. C. H. Spurgeon, in his periodical, *The Sword and
Trowel*, of April 1st (ominous date !), 1872, writes—sheltering himself, however, with the preface, " a correspondent says,"—" If I were asked to select
the Cornish parish which contains, in relation to its population, the largest
number of intelligent people, I should at once turn to Mullion."   So that
in a generation the depraved wretches of the Rev. Smith have become the
highly intelligent of the Rev. Spurgeon.   This would argue some force of
character truly, and if the latter eminent divine really means what he says, and
is not poking fun at us in his wonted comical fashion ; or, even if his words
were strictly true, Mullyon folk would, indeed, be an exceptional race.   The
commonly accepted theory is that the bucolic mind does not, as a rule, possess
such quick perceptive powers as that of the working miner or the artizan.

But, in sober sense, I suppose there is about as much real truth in the words of one of these historians as there is in those of the other ; and for my own part I cannot help saying that while wrecking has ceased among us, and drunkenness is rare, our people are not free from the two chief faults for which Cornish folk have made themselves conspicuous in Parliamentary returns and courts of law ; and at the same time marks of an intelligence so *superior* to the rest of their fellow county men are so faint, that I for one have failed, during a residence of ten years, to observe them.

A number of families seemed to have remained pretty much in the same spot for generations, and Surnames which occur in the parish registers as far back as they go, viz., 1598, may be traced down to the present time, such as Carter, Curtys, Harrey, Kempthorne, Tonken, Triggs, and many others, while Mullyon Folk have always been noted for their love of Classical and Scriptural words as Christian names. Abraham, Aserath, Demetrius, Dionysius, Erasmus, Hannibal, Hercules (which having been modified into Herklous, now crops up as Archelaus), Isa, Jeremiah, Joel, Renatus, Selina, Theophilus, Thyrza, &c., are still in use.

George, Thomas, and Williams, are so plentiful at present as surnames, that some sobriquet is often added to distinguish the individual. This is the more necessary when the christian, as well as the surname, is the same. There are now no less than six or seven Thomas Thomases living in the parish.

This leads me to mention some curious cognomens I find in the registers. In the Register of Burials, in the year 1762, appear the following entries :

> John James, *alias* Gilley, March 5.
> John James, *alias* Cazoose, July 9.
> John James, *alias* Casouse the younger, September 3.

Now, doubtless, all these three aliases are local ; they are taken from the place of abode of each individual. There are several of this nature in our Registers, thus :

> Grace, daughter of Peter Mundy (*alias* Foss), September 8th, 1765.
> Edward, son of Edward and Mary James (*alias* Tangey), November 4, 1804.
> Grace Harris (*alias* Ellis), April 3, 1805.

Foss meaning the ditch ; *Tangey* being a place so named near Carminow, Tangey meaning under the hedge ; and *Ellis*—hal-las—the green moor. So John James, *alias* Gilley, is John James, of the grove, *celli* ; and *Casous* points to the district lying in S. Keverne parish, between Crousa Downs and the Black Head, the inhabitants of which locality are to this day known as the Casousers, and hence these Jameses are known to have come.

Such a custom was common enough in Tonkin's time, while also "nicknames" were no less frequent than they are now. Here is a list of the present nicknames of the inhabitants of the several parishes in Mêneag, *Meneâg* itself being the name locally applied—and not by reason of any ecclesiastical or civil arrangement—to the whole of the promontory which is bounded on the north by Helford Creek and the Loe.

LANDEWEDNACK, OR LIZARD	*ONIONS.*
GRADE	*GEESE.*
S. RUAN	*DUCKS.*
S. KEVERNE	*ROMANS.*
S. ANTHONY	*PIGS.*
MANACCAN	*SWEETS.*
S. MAWGAN	*OWLS.*
S. MARTYN	*KITES.*
CURY	*CROWS.*
GUNWALLOE	*JACKDAWS.*
MULLYON	*GULLS.*

These give rise to many a harmless joke or repartee, which often act as lubrication to conversational machinery. Thus, a Lizard man, thinking to "roast" a Mullyon neighbour, remarked to the company, "Wisht people they are over to Mullyon, I was over there the other day and they was looking wisht, sure 'nuff, the gulls was—quite wearisome and sad they was looking—they'd fairly got tears in their eyes they had." "Iss! an no wonder, I should think,'' retorted the Mullyon man, "when they'd got a Lizard onion before their eyes."

A "foreigner," by which is meant an "up-the-country man," had better be careful how he meddles with these *sobriquets*. It would hardly be safe for such an one to ask a S. Ives man what they commonly did with hakes, for instance, in that picturesque little town.

But now as to the meaning of this word Casous. "The Lizard" I believe simply to signify "The Lazar's abode," as well here as Lezardrieux (Lizard-on-the-Trieux), on the opposite coast of Brittany, at Wymondham in Norfolk, and at Lizarea Wartha, and Wollas, in Gwendron parish.

"Now when that dreadful disease, the leprosy, was introduced into Europe, towards the end of the 12th century, by the returning Crusaders, those who were affected by it were subject to certain regulations. They were obliged to live in communities apart from the people, the only trade they were permitted to follow was that of rope-making, and they were known by the name of "Lazars," in allusion to Lazarus, the beggar, full of sores, of the parable. The horror inspired by the leper has, in Brittany, survived the leprosy, and has attached itself to that of rope-making, which was peculiar to lepers. Rope makers are to this day looked upon with contempt and called "kakous," or " cagous,"* that is, persons dwelling apart."

Now, the Welsh word for those set apart as hateful—to be avoided, is "casaus." Borlase, in his Cornish vocabulary, gives "casaus" as "odious," but says the word is Armoric. " Casadow " is used in the old Cornish Drama with a similar signification. And here we have a certain community living in Lizard district spoken of with contempt to this very day (whether rightly or wrongly, with justice or from mere tradition, is another matter), as "casousers." I think the inference as to the origin and meaning of the word is plain.

Certain it is that from whatever cause, whether it be owing to the perpetually salt moistness of the atmosphere, or whether it be something in the water due to the volcanic origin of the subsoil, that skin affections, of an ephemeral character, truly, but whether contagious, or not, is still a moot point, are prevalent throughout the whole of the district.

Query. Was ever the well in Park Venton, on Tremenhehe farm, the water of which was always formerly used, as tradition says, for baptisms, resorted to as the well of S. Meen was, in Brittany, for the cure of such diseases?

---

* Jephson's walking tour in Brittany, in which see also account of the tragic ceremonies with which the poor leper was "declared" and cut off from social intercourse.

ANCIENT REMAINS.

N what is now called Clahar Garden estate, one of the farms belonging to Lord Robartes, the name of which would probably be more correctly rendered *Claiar Cairn*, or *Cleyar Carn*, a Barrow, thirty-six feet in diameter, was removed some time ago, for the purpose of agriculture, in which, surrounded by an outer circle of stones, four urns were discovered, varying from a foot to four inches in height. One of these urns, which were all of a coarse make, and ruddy brown hue, contained ashes, while a quantity of ashes were also found scattered in the vicinity of the other three. A number of flints were also dug up at the same spot. There is a plan of the cairn and also a good engraving of the urns given in Mr. Borlase's "Nænia Cornubiæ," p. 223, *et seq.*

At Angrouse, Mr. Peter Williams, the proprietor, has of late reclaimed and brought under cultivation a considerable portion of the "Morrops," *i.e.*, croft and pasture land on the edge of the cliffs. While this was being effected the workmen came upon a pile of stones, thirty-five feet in diameter, and between three and four feet high. The centre of this pile was considerably lower than its outer edge, and near the western part of this, covered with layers of flat stones, was found a pit about four feet by two, and two feet deep, cut in the solid rock. Herein were discovered a number of calcined bones, the remains of an urn, of which some portions bore the marks of fire ; a bronze dagger, about 6½ inches in length, with three pivots; and a globular bit of mundic, about 1½ inches in diameter. It has been supposed that this last was used as a "strike-a-light" for the funeral pyre.

Another tumulus was afterwards opened on this estate, also on the cliff, and about 400 yards from the former. This, however, was entirely of earth, about thirty feet across and four feet high. In the centre, under a thin flat stone, was found an urn, with its mouth upwards, and filled with ashes and burnt human bones.

On Predannack Downs a third mound has lately been searched. On the 11th of November, 1871, the present writer formed one of a party in its exploration. It is situated at the entrance from the Downs to Hervan Lane on its southern side. "The Tumulus, in this instance," I quote "Nænia Cornubiæ," p. 240, "was about four feet in height, and had a diameter of forty-two feet. It was surrounded by a ring of stones set on edge, but otherwise was entirely composed of earth. At a depth of scarcely three feet, in the exact centre, the pickaxe struck into a substance much harder than the rest of the mound. This turned out to be a bed of white clay common to the country around, which had been artificially heaped up as a protection to a quantity of calcined bones and ashes. This deposit on being uncovered presented a most curious appearance. There being no covering stone the fibres and roots from the surface had found their way to the bones. These had been originally contained in a small urn, but the roots had caused them to expand and to burst this vessel. The conglomerate when removed measured about nine inches in thickness, by one foot six inches in diameter; it had much the appearance, and quite the consistency of hard Cavendish tobacco; and round the edges of the mass were found adhering the small broken fragments of the vessel, which to the otherwise unprotected ashes had served the purpose of a kist. The urn must have been of the cylindrical shape, about seven inches high. It was carelessly baked, but ornamented with the chevron pattern."

Later in the same day we visited two other tumuli, on the rising ground to the northward, across Hayl Kymbro, but found they had been already opened and their contents removed. The small stones of which these mounds are formed still shew the effects of the action of fire. Near these tumuli, in a N.W. direction, are many remains of *robins* still plainly visible.

C

PREDANNACK CROSS.

This ancient monument is to be found near the village of Predannack
Wartha, in the south corner of a field, through which the church path runs to
Mullyon.   Itself, a block of granite, it stands on a pedestal a foot in thickness, and four feet by three feet two inches "oblong square."   The shaft of the
cross is ten inches thick, and one foot, two inches, broad ; the diameter of its
circular head being two feet across.   The height from pedestal to the top is
five feet four inches.   A broad raised Cross, with ends expanded, is shewn on
the Western face, and on the reverse a narrow incised one appears, surrounded
by an incised circle.

In the year 1852 it was found that accident or wanton hands had removed
the cross from its socket, and it was discovered, lying face downward, in a
neighbouring ditch.   Thereupon, some good people, unwilling that the sacred
symbol should long lie thus neglected, formed a party of volunteers, who, furnished with ropes and levers, proceed to the spot, and with a hearty yet
reverent good-will, hauled out the ancient relic from its ignominious position,
and once more set it upright in its former place, firmly securing it in its socket
with metal wedges.

ANCIENT CHAPEL AT PREDANNACK.

This once stood in what is now the farm yard of the manor.   There is no
record of its dimensions, and the remains of a benatura and some pieces of
window mullion, are hardly sufficient to fix its date.   Within a few yards is a
plot of ground called Jarine (*dzharn*, a garden), now an orchard, which was
formerly a burial ground, and there is a legend connected with it which would
have suited the pages of Sir Henry Spelman, in his "History and Fate of
Sacrilege."   It is said, and commonly believed, that if ever the ground in this
enclosure is disturbed, some member of the occupants of the estate dies before
the year is out.   As a fact, it was last broken in the year 1820, and the same
year a Mullyon man was murdered on his way home from Helston.   Long
ago, and yet, perhaps, within a century, three men, who were lepers, escaping
shipwreck, found their way to Predannack ; two of them died of disease and
exposure, and were buried in one corner of Jarine.   The other recovered,
having taken care, it is said, always to sleep among the sheep.

A curious little relic, whether connected in any way with the old chapel it is impossible to say, was picked up in the Morryps, by Mr. John Thomas, the present occupier of Predannack. One day, in 1871, as he was taking shelter under a large rock from a passing shower, his eye lighted on a bit of metal at his feet, and on taking it up he discovered it to be a small signet or seal of bronze, bearing in its centre the monogram, I.H.C., surmounted by a cross, having a bifurcated base, and the legend running round it—VANGIES TOI— "Jesus avenge thee."

ANCIENT CHAPEL AT TRENANCE.

There is a tradition which points to an old chapel that once stood in the valley leading down to Porthmellin, just below the present farm house at Trenance Veor, but there are now no remains of it to be found, and its very site is almost forgotten. The spiritual needs of the people of Mullyon must have been well looked after at one time with these three chapels, besides the parish church, that is if all, as is possible, existed together. And there was then but one form of religion. The reflection can hardly be avoided: how sad it is that Church and Preaching House are not at one in worship now in this dear old Cornish land of ours. The frequenters and upholders of both Church and Preaching House surely *mean* the same thing—to live a Godly and a christian life, to speak the truth in love, to discountenance sin and lawlessness at all hazards, and, if needs be, patiently suffer for the truth's sake. Until such a happy state shall again be realised, our boasted motto " One and all " must be a reproach to us rather than a ground of boasting.

ANCIENT CHAPEL AT CLAHAR GARDEN.

RAMBLE NO. 2.

On our way hither we will take another ramble, leaving the Church-town by the South-eastern road, which joins the direct road from Helston to the Lizard at Penhayl, on past Vounder farm-house to the Cairn. Here, in this quarry, you see the beginning of the true serpentine, which extends hence eastward and southward for about four miles. Mount the rising ground at the back of the quarry, and, provided the atmospheric conditions are at all favourable, you shall not behold so fine a prospect, so extensive and varied a land-and-sea view, for many and many a mile. I have been on this spot in company with those who have travelled far in the East Indies and in the West, in Australia, the Pacific, and the Mediterranean, and who have confessed that this panorama equalled any thing of a like nature they ever beheld. One summer evening I was here with a dear friend who had resided long in Switzerland and the Tyrol. It happened to be a more than ordinarily glorious sunset. " I've seen the sun rise," said he, " often from the Righi ; I've seen him set from many a peak in many a plain, but I never before saw anything to equal this." Now let us go on through the hamlet of Meaver, and the farmyard of Clahar, towards Fenton Ariance ; but first I wish you to look at a very curious formation which Arch'laus Harry, one of our notabilities, laid bare, not long ago, whilst quarrying—we shall find it in the next field, to the eastward. Note though, in passing, what we have here in the stile—a twenty-eight pounder !—how came it here, in the name of all that's warlike ? What an ignominious position for such a noble weapon ! Could you not write an ode to it or on it ? Well, here is this bit of rock, and if you compare it in position with its surroundings does it not look for all the world like the mouth of an extinct volcano. Can you not imagine those perpendicular striæ, as smooth as if wrought by a huge planing tool, to have been formed by the continuous upward rush of flame and detritus ? Serpentine is supposed to be of volcanic origin, I believe. Now let us down through the fields and lanes towards the silver spring farm—Venton Ariance. Why, here are signs of trees too— actually a decent sized and wide-spreading oak. Be not surprised ; Goonhilly was once a forest, and the massive old oak seats in Mullyon church were grown at Kynance. Further down the valley, and cross the stream that comes down from Clahar water, notice the growth of those splendid ferns — the hart's tongue must be some of them four feet long if they are an inch,— and this lovely and thickly wooded *cwm*, along which runs our road to Helston. Would you imagine that you are scarcely more than a mile from the sea. Just across is a field called " Tretharrap," a name that has long puzzled the etymologists, and the readers of " Notes and Queries." These trees would, most of them, in winter, present to you a remarkable appearance, for, in proof of the continuous moistness of the atmosphere, the lichens hang from their every branch and twig, as if they were provided with a coat of fur, or, as dependant rime. I have gathered it three inches long from off the boughs. But here we are at Clahar Garden. With permission from Mr. Thomas (for all the foot-paths are long ago obliterated), we will cross over the hillock on which the cairn and tumuli before described were found, and down into the wood where the remains of the old chapel are still to be seen. Here it is, with the trees and ivy growing up through its remaining bit of wall close to a small tributary to the stream which taking its rise on Goonhilly, finds its exit to the sea at Poljew.

Some have supposed this chapel to have been dedicated to S. Clare, but why S. Clare is connected with this chapel is not very evident, except on the supposition that Clare and Clahar are synonymous, and this is by no means clear. St. Malo's Moor is not very far off, only just a little further down the valley, at Chypons. The external dimensions of the chapel are : Length, 21 feet ; breadth, 14 feet. The walls are 2 feet 3 inches thick. There are signs of an entrance on the South side, 3 feet wide, and about four feet from the Eastern end ; and of another in the north, 8 feet from the western end ; but its width it is now impossible to calculate. The building is rapidly falling to pieces, and before long will be but a mere heap of stones.

I may mention here another small relic which I found in the church whilst removing some of the rotten flooring. It was lying on the sandy surface beneath (together with a few human bones, and two or three lead pencils, really sticks of soft lead, three and four inches long, and rather less than a quarter of an inch in diameter), and it consisted of a small ink or colour bottle, of an unmistakeably ancient glass, with the neck and mouth inverted after the fashion of our modern pocket ink-holders.

MULLYON CHURCH.

ELAN, or S. Melanus, was, we have seen the name always formerly given in the law reports and in ecclesiastical returns to this parish, and I think, upon a little consideration, we shall conclude, together with Alban Butler, Oliver, and others, in identifying S. Melanus with S. Malo, the individual in whose memory this Church was dedicated, and whose name takes now with us the form "Mullyon."

S. Malo, it would appear, was a man of many *aliasses*—as Mellonus or Melanus, Melanius, Melan, Melonius Britannus, Mellion, Maclovius, Maclou Machutus, Mahut, Menvennus, Mawes and Meen—perhaps some others also. He is to be found in our English Church Kalendar as Machutus on the 15th November, although we keep our parish feast at Mullyon on the 6th of that month—the orientation of the body of the Church, after allowing for difference of compass "Variation" agrees with the latter date—and curiously enough the feast of S. Melan* is observed at Rennes, in Brittany, also on the 6th of November, although in the Roman Kalendar his name occurs on the 6th of January.

The history of S. Malo, according to Ussher, Colgan, Alban Butler and others, runs thus :—He was born early in the sixth century of rich and noble parents, in the valley of Llan Carvan, in Glamorganshire, and was baptized by S. Brendan, then Abbat of a monastery in South Wales. While yet a youth he was sent to be educated into Ireland, where he made rapid progress

---

* *Legenda Sanctorum* of Bishop Grandison speak of Melanius as King of Cornwall. Thus in the legend of S. Mylor "Sanctus Melorus *Meliani* Cornubiæ *Regis* filius, &c."

MULLYON CHURCH.

From a Photograph by J. Beringer.

in learning and virtue. Being ordained priest, he was soon after elected Bishop by the suffrages of the people ; but he declined that dignity and retired in company with his cousin-german S. Sampson, a Cornishman, into Brittany. Here he put himself under the direction of a recluse of the name of Aron, at whose request he went and preached to the heathen on the opposite Coast, and whom he afterward succeeded in the government of the monastery near Aleth. About the year 541 he was elected Bishop of this city, and here he remained until his enemies, roused to jealousy by his reputation and virtues, thrust him out of his Episcopal throne. During his exile many were induced by his holy example to imitate the purity of his life, and others were moved by his exhortations to shun the dangers of the troubled ocean of this world in the retirement of a life of meditation. He was permitted once more to return to the scene of his episcopal labours, and to reward his persecutors with forgiveness and his benediction. Being overtaken by a mortal sickness he gave up his soul to his Maker, lying on sack cloth and ashes, about the year 570.

John, surnamed de la Grille, Bishop of Aleth, in 1150 removed the seat of his see to the island on which the monastery of S. S. Aron and Malo stood. Thither the remains of the latter were translated, Aleth was deserted of its inhabitants, and thenceforward the town which soon sprung up and covered the island, took his name—S. Malo.

The probability of Mullyon being none other than S. Malo is heightened by the fact of the frequent intercourse which, without doubt, existed about that time between the inhabitants of this part of Cornwall and those who dwelt in the north of Brittany ; and while many of our parishes preserve the names of Saints of Irish extraction, almost all those which skirt Mount's Bay are dedicated to persons who under similar circumstances to S. Malo retired into Brittany, particularly that part of it which is now called 'Côtes du Nord' thus—

S. Paul near Penzance, is not the Apostle Paul but S. Pol, Bishop of Leon, a native of Cornwall, and, like S. Malo, cousin-german of S. Sampson, Bishop of Dol.[1]

---

1. Butler's lives. Vol. 1. p. 341., and Oliver's Monast : Sup : notes.

Madron, is S. Paternus, or Madiern (Welsh Padern, see below under Cury).
Dr. Oliver after collating several authorities concludes that Madron, or as
he is locally called Madderne (or as in Chancery Proceedings *Temp. Eliz.*
Madderen) is none other than S. Paterne Bishop of Avranches in 6th
century.

Gulval is S. Gudwal who was born in Wales, was Abbat of Plecis, came into
Cornwall, afterwards crossed to Brittany, succeeded S. Malo in the
Bishopric of Aleth, and died about the beginning of the 7th century.[2]

Breage, S. Breaca, according to Borlase and Leland an Irish disciple of S.
Patrick; but it should be remembered that S. Brieuc or Brioc, a man of
illustrious extraction, a native of Great Britain, most probably of Cornwall, crossed to Brittany when he was about 20 years of age, A.D. 429,
was there ordained priest, returned to his own country, converted his
parents, and with their aid built a famous Church called Grandellan.
The Monastery of S. Brieuc in Brittany was erected into a Bishopric,
A.D. 844.[3]

Gunwalloe, S. Winwolaus, or Guingualoc, of noble Welsh extraction, educated
by S. Budoc (who was also a British Abbot) in the monastery of Lande-
vedneck in Brittany, of which he was afterwards the Abbot. He died
A.D. 529.[4]

Cury, S. Corentin, as a young man passed several years in the forest of Ploe-
Madiern=The Parish of S. Madern. He was the first Bishop of
Quimper in Brittany.[5]

Landewednack, "Grullo, count of Cornuailles, in which the Abbey of Lande-
vedneck is situated in the Diocese of Quimper-Corentinus, gave the lands
and was at the expense of the foundation of this famous monastery."[6]

And we have here 'The Lizard' answering to Lezardrieux (The Lizard on
the Trieux) in north Brittany, and this parish of Mullyon, Melan, or Malo.

Again S. Mellion Church (S. Melanus, *Oliver*) near Southill in east Cornwall,
is dedicated to S. Melan or Malo, Southill Church being dedicated to his
companion and cousin-german S. Sampson; and here in Mullyon we have in

---

2. Butler, Vol. 1. p. 752.   3. Butler, Vol. 1. p. 549.   4. Oliver, p. 439, and Butler, Vol. 1. p. 293.
5. Oliver, Sup: p. 37.   6. Butler, Vol. 11. p. 1034.

Clahar garden estate, and near the remains of the ancient chapel, two fields
that are called 'S. Malo's moor' to this day, and on the same estate (let this go
for what it may be worth) two other fields named 'Sampson's crofts.'

The Church is a plain building of the latter part of the 15th century, but
possessing many interesting features. It consists of nave, chancel, N. and S.
aisles, Western Tower, and S. Porch, of which the following are the dimensions internally :—

Length of Nave	42 feet.
Width of Do.	17 feet.
Length of Chancel	14 feet.
Width of Do.	17 feet.
Length of N. Aisle	53 feet 10 in.
Width of Do.	12 feet 4 in.
Length of S. Aisle	54 feet 9 in.
Width of Do.	10 feet 6 in.
Height of nave and aisles to ridge	24 feet and 22 feet.
Height of Tower from base to top of parapet	42 feet.
Internal measurement of Tower	11 feet × 7 feet 10.
External ditto	16 feet × 15 feet.
S. Porch	7 ft. 8 wide × 9 ft. deep.

The Sacrarium was rebuilt eastwards to the depth of 7 feet 6 inches by
Rev. F. Gregory, in 1840.

The present structure evidently occupies the site of a much older church,
probably one of the 12th century. The dripstone moulding, with its charac-
teristic terminations, which is built into the present later tower, is of this date;
as also are the remains of a polished purbeck marble memorial slab, with a
raised floriated cross upon it, which now lies in the floor of the N. aisle.
Some portions of Early English window jambs, that have lately turned up, the
crucifix built into the tower over the lower western window, the abaci of the
Tower arch, and the fact that the Tower itself is of a different orientation to
the nave and chancel—all go to point to an earlier edifice. This indeed
appears to have been the history of almost all our Cornish parish churches—

D

rebuilt in the 15th century on older sites, and retaining in many places remnants of the former building of a first pointed, and in some cases, a Norman type.

Of the present Church at Mullyon the nave and S. aisle appear to be the earlist portions, the N. aisle being added probably not long before the Tower was built. The pillars which separate the latter from the nave (there are 6 on either side) are of better stone and better workmanship than the southern row, and the arches are somewhat loftier. A portion of the S. wall, that between the porch and the priest's door was rebuilt in 1691. The Tower, built by Robert Luddre, in 1500, is a massive structure of three stages, having a good newel staircase in the N. W. corner. Composed as it is of large blocks of granite and hornblende, it is curious to notice how infinitely better the latter has stood the wear and tear of the weather than the former, which is commonly supposed to be the most durable of building material. The Tower is curiously enough built on to, against, and not into or with the western walls of the W., N. and S. aisles. It contains four bells, which were, replacing older ones, cast at Hayle Foundry, in 1828, Peter Willey and Hanibal Shepherd being Church Wardens.

Extract from Parish Book—

"1828 to Lady Day, 1829,

To 4 new bells and clappers, stocking, &c....£187 16 1½
"Received for old bells and iron 171 18 3

£ 15 17 10½

The windows, with the exception of the Eastern windows of the aisles, which are four-light eliptic-headed, and the upper tower lights, are poor and without tracery.

The roof of both nave and aisles is of the common Cornish cradle pattern, with carved principals, bosses and wall-plates. On the N. wall-plate of the chancel will be found this legend in raised letters—

"do robert: Luddre op' rfirit a.d. milio.ccccc."

and on the wall-plate of the south chancel aisle, the following in ruder type—

"Hoc opus factum fuit ano domini. M.D."

The old oak seats whose beauty is now more appreciable since they were set up in their proper places, and relieved of their encumbrances of rotting deal by the present Vicar in 1870, are probably unique, being "carved in a manner much superior to those in any other church in the West of Cornwall." —*Blight.* Tradition speaks of their having been wrought from timber grown on what are now Goonhilly and Kynance Downs. If this were the case it will have been from the last remnants of the Nemæan wood, in close proximity to which S. Rumon had as long ago as the 9th century, built his oratory and cell. These seats were probably carved about the time that the roof was made, and they shew signs of having been designed and wrought by four different hands. The treatment of some is very bold, and many are in a very good state of preservation, even after the lapse of 400 years ; the features of some of the figures being as sharp and distinct as on the day on which they were cut. Besides a number of very bold initial letters, and the usual emblems of the crucifixion, may be found in the medallions of the bench ends the heads of Herod and his men of war, of Judas Iscariot, Pontius Pilatus, and his wife Juditha, the mockers at the crucifixion, the soldiers asleep at the tomb, &c. &c. ; and in addition, as was not unfrequently the case with the old carvers—at the instigation of the *secular* doubtless—caricatures of some of the *regular* clergy, and of those in minor orders. And not the least interesting portion of this wood work is to be found in the almost Italian form of some of the designs, remarkable as it is for its thus early appearance in Cornwall. A great number of these bench ends were rescued from destruction and decay in 1870, but rumour speaks of a good deal of pilfering that has been committed, even of late years. The present writer has himself seen a modern photograph of one, whom it is not necessary here to name, leaning on a chair, which contingent circumstances lead him to conclude could have had no other origin than the old carved bench ends from Mullyon church.

At the same time that the remaining seats were cleansed from the accumulated filth of years, and set up in their original places, the lower portion of the rood screen was discovered under the rotten deal pews in the N. aisle. This also has been restored to its former position, and it is hoped that, however much it has suffered from its burial, it may be allowed to remain in its present position and state, unaltered—beautiful even as a wreck, and a token and remembrancer of times when men had a care for God's house as for their own.

Mr. Blight, in his "Churches of West Cornwall," gives a woodcut of "two figures carved in wood, each having one hand raised to bless. One of these, evidently intended for S. Clare, stands at the entrance of an ecclesiastical structure and holds a monstrance in her right hand. These carvings formed part of the roodscreen." This was written previous to the discovery of the roodscreen mentioned above, which is of an earlier date and a totally different character. It may be meant for S. Clare, but it has no connexion with the ancient chapel or the estate named Clahar Garden, for this last is simply the modern rendering of *Cleyr Carn.* They appear to me to be panels of an old chest, perhaps the old church chest, and they now form a front to the Litany stool.

The whole of the carved work in Mullyon Church will be interesting, not only to the architect and the antiquarian, but also to any devout Christian who will not think anything too good to be dedicated to his Master's service; and nothing now should be left undone to preserve these interesting relics from further decay.

Some idea may be formed of the internal state of the Church a few years ago, when the writer states that with his own hands he carted out fifteen wheelbarrow loads of perfectly rotten snuff-like wood, while in 1870 removing the deal sleeping pews which hid the old oak seats. That they should have, in a short time, reached this state of decay, is not wonderful, when the western doorway was built up, the north door was built up, the priest's door was built up, and there was not a window that could let in the air, and the only kind of ventilation the place had was when the Church was opened for service on Sundays.

A parishioner was lately heard to make the remark to a stranger, "Our Church now do smill sa sweet as a rose," leaving the impression on the auditor that there was a time when it did not. At one period it was moreover necessary to protect ones feet by India-rubber goloshes or iron pattens from the frequent pools of water lying in the alleys between the pews. But now we have changed all that. Deo gratias!

In the Porch there exist the remains of a plain Benatura, or holy water Stoup, the well-worn stone front of which tells a tale of a time when people were wont to come to church on other occasions than that of funerals only. Immediately opposite to the 4-centred internal archway of the porch is the Devil's door in the north wall; so called, as legends say, from the ancient custom of opening this door at the time of Baptism to allow of a speedy retreat of the evil spirit to his northern abodes of darkness.

The staircase of the Rood loft has disappeared, but the entrance doorway to the staircase, as well as the exit above, and the aperture through the north wall of the nave, were all brought to light during the reparations of 1870. It was in this doorway that the marble memorial slab was discovered, being turned face inward, and built up into the opening, even as the remains of the church-yard cross, to be mentioned below, was found buried with its head downwards, as if some of our predecessors had, in their mistaken piety, endeavoured to obliterate or hide out of sight, every symbol of our salvation.

There is in the sacrarium wall a modest and well cut brass inscription to the memory of Thomas Flavel, a former Vicar, who held the living for 48 years; and there are also two "superior" mural tablets to successors.

The following is a copy of Flavel's monument :—

> *Thomæ Flavel Clerici*
> *Joh : Flavel : S : T : D : Fil :*
> *Com Sommerseten Nati*
> *Schola Tivert Dev Educati*
> *Col : S : Trinitatus Oxon Alumni A : M :*
> *Ecclæ* { *Mullianensis Vicarii*
> *Ruani Majoris Rectoris*
> *E : D : Petri Exon Prebend :*
> *Hic Deponuntur Exuviæ*
> *Anno ætatis suæ LXXVII*
> *Et Doi Nostri Jes : Chi : 1682.*

> *Earth take thine Earth. my Sin. let Satan havet*
> *The World my goods, my Soul : my God, who gavet*
> *For from these four : Earth ; Satan ; World and God*
> *My flesh ; my Sin, my Goods. my Soul I had.*

The following is on an incised slate now lying in the North Aisle :—

✠ Here lyeth the Body of Robert Priske who died ye 26th day of March in the yeare of our Lord God 1699.

Ætæs suæ 62 yeares.

My sun is set My glas is run
My Life is spent My days are don
Neither witt nor virtue can preuail
Death takes no quarter gives no Bail
Yet I doe hope to see ye day
When death's strong power shall away
Tho' now I lye here in ye dust
Yet surely rise again I must
To meet my Sauiour in ye skey
Goe reader goe prepare to dye.

The Windows at one time must have contained a considerable quantity of stained glass, if they were not wholly filled with it. The few remnants that were left have been carefully collected, and now go to form (missing portions having been supplied) a beautiful subject—The presentation of their costly gifts by the Eastern Magi. This has been placed in a new window of stone work in the East end of the Chancel. The subject, which has been artistically handled, was entrusted to Messrs. Beer and Driffield, of Exeter. The Sacrarium and chancel floor have lately been relaid with floriated encaustic tiles from the manufactory of Mr. W. Godwin, of Lugwardine Works, Hereford.

The head and arms of the old Churchyard Cross were discovered in 1870, turned upside down and inserted in the line of kerb stone which marks the path outside the Western Lych gate. This ancient relic has also been preserved and set up on an appropriate shaft and base, in the usual position, S.E. of the Porch, it bears the following inscription.

TO HIM
WHO RAISED THIS CROSS
AND TO ALL FAITHFUL PEOPLE
PARDON AND PEACE
GRANT O LORD
AMEN.

Within the last few years, besides the internal work already mentioned, the Nave, Chancel, and S. Aisle roofs have been entirely re-slated, and new lead gutters laid down, the bells have been newly set up and the tower repaired and re-pointed, but much is still required to be done, and funds are sorely needed.

It seems more than a pity that the present inhabitants (none of whom, with two or three exceptions, have contributed to the work of keeping their Chùrch from falling to utter decay) should decline not only to meet the current expenses incident to the usual Church Services, but even to keep their Church-yard, their only burial-ground, in decent order.

LIST OF VICARS OF MULLYON.

ROBERT LUDDRE, sometime Provost of Glasney College, Penryn, and who built Mullyon Tower and Church roofs. He is entered in the *Valor Ecclesiasticus* of Bp. Vesey as Vicar ... ... 3rd June 1536

ALEXANDER DAW, was Vicar in 1549

THOMAS FLAVEL, was Vicar for 48 years, having been instituted in 1634, and dying 1682

WILLIAM TONKEN, ... died 1720

JOHN WILLS ... ... ,, 1750

HUGH TONKEN, of Trenance, in this Parish, Rector of Lidford, in Devon, 1747. Vicar of this Parish, and Chaplain on board H.M. Ship 'Vanguard' in Plymouth Sound 1755 ... ... died 1760

NICHOLAS CARKEET, ... ,, 1780

RICHARD VIVIAN, sometime fellow of Exeter College, Oxford, resigned 1797

ROOPE ILBERT ... ... ,, 1798

THOMAS ASH ... ... died 1812

EDWARD WARNEFORD ... ... resigned 1831

THOMAS LOVELL BLUETT ... ... died 1834

FRANCIS GREGORY ... ... ,, 1853

HENRY BAWDEN BULLOCKE ... ... resigned 1865

EDMUND GEORGE HARVEY ... ...

For extracts from Churchwardens' Books see Appendix B.

RAMBLE No. 3.

—

LEAVING Church Town by the foot-path that leads to Le Frowder, and on past Merres in the direction of Polurrian, we pass along a narrow lane, in which the rare fern *Lanceolatum* is to be found. *Asplenium Marinum* reaches a very luxuriant growth in the neighbouring cliffs, and about the Cove flourish the Golden Samphire, the Lady's Finger, and the Tree Mallow. For a complete botanical list of the whole peninsula of the Meneag—this district of Leguminosæ, I cannot do better than refer the reader to " A week at the Lizard " of the Rev. C. A. Johns, as also for a catalogue of birds observed, both of which are compiled with evident care. In the vicinity of Polurrian Cove, on either side and on the edge of the cliffs, the remains of many a storm-lost mariner have found a last resting place, for it is only of a comparatively recent date—a little more than half a century (by an Act of Parliament brought in by the late Mr. Davies Gilbert) that greater care has been manifested for the bodies of the wreck-drowned, by their being interred in the Parish Burial Grounds.

Ascend the hill to the southward and we come upon another deserted mine —Huel Fenwick. This shaft was dug to the depth of about 30 fathoms, an engine erected, the " bob " of which was " heaved " on 7th December, 1853, but in the following year, no ore making its appearance, the " concern was knocked." Miners, however, still hold to the belief that good copper is to be found not very far off.

On further, past the hoar rock—*carrag lûz*—the flag staff, and the coast-guard look-out, and hence you look down upon our principal fishing ground.

Here it is, and on the adjoining head of Henscath, that the Huer stands in the months of Autumn, watching with anxious eye for the approach of a "school" of fish, or to direct the boats below whilst "shooting a seine."

PILCHARD FISHERY.

The pilchard fishery here, although on no extensive scale, has been at most times attended with fair profits to the adventurers, excepting in the seasons between 1859 and 1864, during which period not a single fish was taken.

There are now eight seines employed, of which five are the property of Messrs. Bolitho, Coulson, and Co. ; Edward Batten, Esq., owns one ; and Messrs. Trahair and Co., of Newlyn, keep two seines. The season commences usually about the beginning of September, and continues on till late in December, the summer fishery having been discontinued many years ago. The autumn fishery was commenced in 1823, and has been carried on ever since. The Mullyon Farmers also once speculated with a seine, but relinquished their venture in 1832. The mode of enclosing the pilchard has been so often and so minutely described, that it is unnecessary for me to repeat it here. I would, however, for an elaborate and succinct account of the Fisheries of Mounts Bay, refer to a series of papers which appeared in the *Royal Cornwall Gazette* of February and March, 1850, under the well-known initials, R. Q. C.

The manner of paying the men employed is curious, and should be noted. With us at Mullyon, it is at present, thus : —Each Huer receives 17 shillings per week and every twentieth dozen of the fish. The shooters, or those who pay out the net, get 10s. 6d., and the crew 9s. per week ; and these last together divide amongst them one quarter part of the whole catch, which is thus apportioned :—the two shooters, a share and half a share each ; the master of the cock boat and the bowman, a share and a quarter each ; and the remainder of the crew, a share a piece. In addition to this, the shooters receive two pence each ; and the master of the cockboat and the bowman, one penny each on every hogshead of the owners' share of the fish.

There is an error in "A Week at the Lizard" which requires correction. The Author says, p. 37, third edition, "Experienced hands can detect a shoal many miles from the shore, by the difference of colour produced in the water,

E

as well as by unusual flights of sea birds. The excitement now becomes very great ; labourers are summoned from the harvest fields ; women finish off their household work in haste, and all are in eager anticipation of a catch on a grand scale. The seine boats are hauled down, manned and loaded with their nets in all haste, and proceed to the particular spot where experience has taught the fishermen they will stand the best chance of ' shooting the seine ' with advantage."

Few fish would be caught if this plan were adopted. The fact is, as is well known, men and nets, in the boats, afloat, are kept in constant readiness to " shoot " at a moment's notice. I have known but six minutes to have elapsed between the huer's first sighting the fish and the completion of the process of shooting the seine and enclosing them. This occurred to a seine of Messrs. Bolitho's, 28th September, 1866.

Two or three words in connection with the Pilchard fishery seem to demand more attention than has yet been given them as regards their meaning— " Huer," not hewer as it is sometimes wrongly spelt, is evidently from the Norman French, and signifies one whose business it is to cry or raise an alarm. Seine is, doubtless, derived originally from the Greek. Thus, S. Matthew, chap. xiii, v. 47, "The kingdom of Heaven is like unto a net "—*sagene*—so in the Vulgate, " Sagena "—Anglo-saxon segne, now sean or more correctly " seine," pronounced as the name of the French river ; but what is " Heva," the cry that is used on the approach of a shoal of fish and the shooting of a seine? Is it a mere exclamation of joy—a sort of Io ! Hymen ! Io ! Bacche ! &c., or can it be in any way deduced from the following fantastic legend, which is given by Bernardin de Saint Pierre ? He is writing of Havre, his native place, of the river Seine and of Cap Le Hêve.

"The Seine, the daughter of Bacchus and nymph of Ceres, had followed into the land of the Gauls the goddess of wheat, where she was seeking all the earth over for her daughter Proserpine. When Ceres had terminated her wanderings, the Seine begged of her as a reward for her services, the meadows through which the river at present flows. The goddess consented, and granted moreover that wine should grow wherever the daughter of Bacchus planted her feet. She left then the Seine upon these shores, and gave her as her com-

panion and follower the nymph Héva, who was bidden to watch beside her for
fear she might be carried away by some god of the sea, as her daughter
Proserpine had been by the god of Hades.   One day, while the Seine was
amusing herself on the sands, in quest of shells, and when she fled with loud
cries before the blue sea waves, which sometimes wetted her feet, Héva, her
companion, discovered under the water the white locks, the empurpled visage,
and the azure robe of Neptune.   The god had come from the Orcades after a
great earthquake, and was traversing the shores of the ocean, examining with
his trident whether their foundations had been shattered.   On seeing him, Héva
shrieked loudly, and at her warning cry, the Seine immediately fled towards
the meadows.   But the sea-god had also descried the nymph of Ceres, and
moved by her brightness and charming mien, he drove his sea-horses in swift
pursuit.   Just as he was on the point of overtaking her, she cried upon
Bacchus her father, and Ceres her mistress.   Both heard her ; and as Neptune
stretched forth his arm to seize her, all the body of the Seine dissolved into
water ; her green veil and vestments, which the winds fluttered before her, were
changed into emerald waves, she was transformed into a river of the same
colour, which still finds a pleasure in winding through the scenes she had
loved in her days of nymphhood : but what is best worthy of notice is, that
Neptune, despite the metamorphosis, never ceased to love her, as is also said
of the river Alphæus with regard to the fountain Arethusa.   But, if the god of
ocean has preserved his passion for the Seine, the Seine still cherishes her
antipathy to him.   Twice a day he pursues her with awful roar ; and each
time the Seine flies from him into the green inlands, ascending towards her
source, contrary to the natural course of rivers, and separates her green from
the cerulean billows of the ocean."

"Héva died of sorrow, for the loss of her mistress.   But the Nereids, to
reward her for her fidelity, raised to her memory, on the shore, a tomb of black
and white stones, which are visible from a great distance.   By a celestial
artifice, they also enclosed in them an echo, that Héva, after her death, might
both by sight and hearing forewarn the sailors of the danger of the sea.   This
tomb is yonder precipitous mountain, composed of funereal strata of black and
white stones.   It still bears the name of Héva."

I fear the above suggested derivation is, however, rather ingenious than probable. "Héva" would be more simply evolved from the Celtic "Helfa" —*a draught of fishes.*

Our neighbours at Cadgwith and the Lizard, cry "Hubba"; but we, with S. Ives folk (and they are most likely to be correct) shout "Héva!"

The pages of *The Mullyon Gull* record an incident connected with the Mullyon pilchard fishery, thus :—

Orat qui laborat.

How the Parson Caught his Fish on Christmas Day.

A TRUE STORY.

"All on ye shores of Mullyon Cove,
　When sumer daies ben gon,
'Tis iollie to spye ye pilcharde bryghte
　Y sparklinge in ye sonne."

OLD SONG.

On Christmas morn, in sixty-nine,
　Not late, tho' left i'the lurch,
The Parson, he, with his Quiristers three,
　Was on his way to Church.

"Look out! look out! my Quiristers!
　Look out! look out!" quoth he,
" For the people all run to find out the fun
　Whatever it may be."

" Here's Peter running down the lane—
　Here's Ritchie, Sam, and John,"—
" Heva! heva!" they all cry out,
　" Come, lev' us all be gone."

" We can't *all* go," the Parson said
　" I may not go with ye,
I've others, sure, in bulk to cure,
　Than the fishes o' the sea."

" We may'nt all go," the Parson said
　" Ye're fishermen, and cry
Heva! heva! when pilchards come,
　But a fisher of men am I."

"Therefore, good John, while at my work,
   Busy as I shall be,
While ye're afloat, and I'm at Church,
   I will remember ye."

They hied them down unto the cove—
   Let those rejoice that win,
For full seines three were shot i' the sea,
   And the pilchards were therein.

"There's heaps o' pilchurs now," cries Tom,
   "There's a passel o' pilchurs now,
There's hunderds o' hos-geads in William's net,
   And tummals under our bow."

"As purty a sight as ever I seed,"
   Said John, "of a Christmas day,—
But hark to me a minute, my dears,
   And mind what I do say—

The passon goin' to Church this morn,
   Said he'd remember we ;
So now, to kip things straight, say I,
   Lev' us remember he."

And then they took of the pilchards bright
   In baskets to the town,
And at the Vicarage door they laid
   Their glitt'ring burden down.

"Well done ! well done ! my fishers bold !"
   The Parson then did say,
"'Tis well you see, both for you and me
   To labour and to pray."

Now let us descend once more to Porthmellin, the spot "distinguished by its coves, rocks, island, and sandy shore for ever white with ocean foam." But first endeavour to take in and comprehend the scene before you—the stern and rugged cliffs, the glass-green and pellucid waters, the island peacefully reclining on its watery bed, and the ever varying lights and shadows hovering and playing over all.

"Some time before small pox was extirpated," quoth the sage Professor Diogenes Teufelsdröch, "there came a new malady of the spiritual sort on Europe: I mean the epidemic, now endemical, of view-hunting. Poets of old date, being privileged with senses, had also enjoyed external nature; but chiefly as we enjoy the chrystal cup which holds good or bad liquor for us; that is to say, in silence or with slight incidental commentary; never, as I compute, till after the *Sorrows of Werter*, was there man found who would say: Come, let us make a description! Having drunk the liquor, let us eat the glass! Of which endemic the Jenner is unhappily still to seek."

Who could attempt a description of Mullyon Cove after this? Let us go down and take a boat, and on your way note that peculiar throw-down of stones, some of them as square cut as if with a tool for building. How came they there in such fantastic array? We will take a cruise along under the cliffs, for until you have viewed these from the sea you can scarce be said to have really seen them. As we row along I will tell you what our crabbers do.

CRAB FISHERY.

Those are the buoys of their store pots, just inside the island, wherein they stow the fish till called for. The crab and lobster fishing begins about the 21st March, provided the weather be suitable, and lasts till Michaelmas; each boat has from 40 to 50 pots, which cost on an average 30s. a dozen. The bait they use is all manner of fish, which they either catch in trammels made for the purpose, or purchase of passing boats engaged on the hook-and-line fishery. They do not scruple to use the best of fish for bait. Turbot, brill, surmullet, and salmon, together with coarser sorts, are all cut up for bait. For it is a mistake to suppose that these crustaceæ are, as is nevertheless commonly supposed, undainty feeders. They turn up their noses at stale fish, as we should; nay, they are even more particular, more fastidious, as one might say, in their tastes. Should you have a good fresh fish on Saturday and, not requiring the whole of it for bait, took some on shore and preserved it with as much scrupulous care as you would for your own eating, on the Monday a craw-fish disdains to look at it, a crab will not touch it, and a lobster, if very hungry, might persuade himself to taste it, but it it is just as possible that you would find him sitting on the outside of the pot, contemplating it, and debating in his own mind whether it would agree with him or not.

The crabber visits his pots every day when the state of the sea will allow him, at neap tides on the slack of ebb, and at springs on the flood slack ; and every day, or every other day at the furthest, he changes his bait. First he visits his string of pots that are nearest the shore, in 10 fathoms water ; then the others, until he arrives at his fourth or fifth string, in 20 fathoms. Loss of pots is often occasioned by passing vessels or a gale of wind. Fish are only occasionally otherwise lost, unless indeed a store pot breaks loose. One of our men had missed a pot on an occasion, but recovered it after several days, when he found a small bag attached to it, and in the bag two sixpences, the remaining honesty of the dishonest plunderer had thus compelled him to make some kind of compensation to the owner.

The fish are seldom brought on shore unless bespoke ; but a smack, either from Scilly or Lundy calls every nine or ten days in the season, and takes the whole catch, with others from other places, to Southampton. Four or five dozen of fish per boat is the supply this smack may reckon upon at each visit. Prices vary very much ; but last year 14s. a dozen was given for lobsters, 26s. a dozen for crabs and crawfish, and 2s. 6d. a dozen for she crabs.

I hope you have been admiring the cliffs all this time, for after we have been down a little further off Pigeon ogo and the Rill, I mean to come back to Gue Greze, where I have something else to speak of; but I may tell you here that except the granite uprearing at Tol y Pedn, on the other side of Mounts Bay, you may look in vain for a more splendid bit of cliff between this and the Orkneys.

Is the motion of the boat rather much for your comfort? Then let us ashore.

This is Gue Greze—the curving valley, and here is the soap rock, or, rather, the spot where it was, there is not much remaining.

THE SOAPY ROCK.

The principal ingredients for the manufactory of porcelain, it was long ago known, were to be found in this county, where lead and tin for the glazing, and the best description of clays, lay close along side one another.

The valuable properties of the Soap Rock do not seem to have been fully appreciated, even if known, until the middle of the 18th century; but after the discovery of it in this spot, by Mr. R. Chaffers, in 1755, greater quantities appear to have been raised here, at Gue Greze, or "Corez Cove" as it was then called, than in any other part of Cornwall.

Mr. Richard Chaffers, who was a native of Liverpool, and a contemporary of Josiah Wedgwood, having obtained permission from several land proprietors to quarry or bore for soap rock, made a journey into Cornwall in the year 1755 or thereabouts. After varied attempts, attended with varied success, he at length discovered in this valley a larger quantity of clay than he had found elsewhere, and a cargo of this was speedily shipped for Liverpool. Here, Chaffers, by his perseverance and chemical skill and knowledge, soon succeeded in producing from the soapy clay such excellent specimens of china ware, as fairly to win from the great Wedgwood himself the acknowledgement that he had met with a formidable rival ; " Mr. Chaffers," said he, " beats us in all his colours, and can produce for two guineas what I cannot for five."

Chaffers lived for ten years after this, during which time the works were con-tinued here for a supply of the Kaolin, and he was enabled to mature his operations on his important discovery ; but on his demise, his principal assis-tant, Podmore, having died just before him, commenced the breaking up of this branch of the ceramic act that he had brought so near perfection.

At Mullyon, Mr. Chaffers's foreman of the works was one Gavregan Teppit (whose burial is recorded in our register, 4th June, 1785, "aged about 70 ;" and whose daughter was married to the then Vicar of Mullyon), and several letters of this man to his master are still extant. From these, it may be learnt that in 1756 Teppit had sent "eight tuns and fourteen hundred of sopey-rock to Hail," to be shipped for Liverpool : and so during the years following, the work of raising and sending off the clay was continued, save, perhaps, in the depth of winter. In 1759, he writes, "We have the finest parcel of clay that

was ever seen in Paradock.   There was a man down in October who said he
would give any money for such a parcel."   In 1762 they "could raise half a
tun a day."   In the last three months of 1763 he sends off 32 tons ; and in
his last letter to Mr. Richard Chaffers, dated 28th November, 1765, there is
an account of all monies received and paid by him up to that date.   It must
have been in the following December that Mr. Richard Chaffers died, for
Teppit's next letter, towards the end of January, 1766, is written to Mr.
Hannibal Chaffers, saying he has 20 tons to weigh off, and that there was a
very good vein in sight.   He also describes some copper works which they
had come across, very rich, and bringing £96 a ton.   The last of his letters
is dated December, 1767, when the soap rock works were still being carried on.

Mr. Christian, co-executor of Mr. R. Chaffers, with Mr. Hannibal, is
spoken of as producing large china vases of equal quality with the oriental.
The lease of this mine of soap rock in Gue Greze was sold in 1775 to the
Worcester Porcelain Company, for £500.   The value of the clay had been
about £20 a ton ; the lord's dues being £1 upon every ton when weighed off.

In the extracts from the Duesbury papers (*Art Journal*, 1862, p. 4) we find
that Richard Holdship, on leaving Worcester a few years after his bankruptcy,
offered his services at Derby, and that he was enabled at that time (1764) to
offer soap rock at fair prices to the Derby works.

For much of the preceding account I am indebted to Mr. G. A. Howitt ;
and for a graphic description of Chaffers' journey into Cornwall, and for
more minute particulars connected with the works at this spot, I would refer
to "*Marks and Monograms on Pottery and Porcelain, by W. Chaffers,
London,* 1874.

Mr. J. B. Kempthorne, the present proprietor of Polhormon, in this parish,
has enabled me to add the following with respect to other contemporaneous
works on Predannack Downs, which will show, in some measure, how Holdship was in a position to offer the soap rock at Derby.

About the year 1760 Mr. John Thorneloe, one of the partners in the
Worcester works, visited Mullyon, staying for some weeks in the house of Mr.
Renatus Kempthorne, and accompanied him on the first raising of the soap

F

rock, at Dorose, on Predannack Downs. Thorneloe took with him three
boxes, samples of the clay, from which three sets of china were manufactured.
From 1760 to 1770 the Worcester company, Richard Holdship being, during
portion of that time, one of the partners, worked the quarry (which may still
be seen) by a grant, or simple written agreement. They then, with the
assistance of Mr. R. Kempthorne, obtained a lease, of which an extract is
here given.

"Grant of indenture bearing date 1 January, 1770, by and from Geo. Hunt,
of Lanhydrock, in the county of Cornwall, Esq., to John Wall, William Davis,
Benjamin Blayney, and Renatus Kempthorne, of the parish of Mullion, in
the county of Cornwall, gentlemen, of free liberty and authority to dig in a
certain vein or lode of mineral earth commonly called soapy rock, on Predannack Common, in the parish of Mullion, to break and carry off at their
will for the term of 21 years from the date of the said lease, for the yearly
rent of 10 guineas, and in case of raising a larger quantity than ten tons of
the said mineral earth in any one year, then subject to the payment of 21
shillings for each ton exceeding 10 tons that should be raised, &c., &c."

One of the sets of porcelain above mentioned is now in possession of Mr.
J. B. Kempthorne, and it is quite unique in character and manufacture.

Chaffers's lease of the other works must have been a long one, for when it
was purchased by the Worcester Company, in 1775, there were still 17 years
unexpired, and the mine had already been worked for 20 years.

And now to continue our ramble, let us ascend the hill to the right, and
walk along the edge of the cliff to the Rill and Kynance Cove. Soon after
we reach the summit, we are just over Pigeon Hugo—*Poethon ogo*, the boiling
cave—and may look down a sheer perpendicular rock of dark serpentine to a
depth of 250 feet below, where the water never recedes from the base, and
where, as the name implies, it is almost never at rest. This portion of the
cliff, and that onwards to what is called *The Horse*, are most interesting, precipitous, and rugged, washed and lashed as they are by the tempests of winter into
every fantastic and inconceivable form.

The view from the Rill itself across Mount's Bay is fine, though inferior to
that from Pedn Predannack ; but from this point you may well appreciate the

hopeless state of any vessel becoming embayed in a south-westerly or south south-westerly gale.

From the southern side of the Rill we get the most charming view of Kynance Cove—Kynance with all its varied loveliness, which has so often inspired the pen of the word painter, and the pencil of the artist; whose romantic rocks and sands, and coves and caves, have so frequently been enlarged upon from the time of Charles Littleton, Dean of Exeter, and Dr. Borlase, to the two-penny guide book of the present day, that they can need no further description here.

Moreover, is not Kynance known to every one of a host of "Tourists," who drives the twelve miles out from Helston in the morning with the intention of "doing the Lizard," and having devoted *the whole of three hours* to his arduous task, drives his uninteresting twelve miles back again with the satisfaction, we must fairly suppose, of "having done the Lizard." Don't disturb him, his ignorance to him *is* bliss. In most cases you will find it a thankless office if you undertake to suggest to a "tourist" any other plan than that he has himself worked out by the aid of Murray, or Black, and the Helston 'bus.

I have known of some who have meekly "done the Lizard" remaining, by reason of the weather, during their allotted three hours, within the four walls of the by no means capacious parlour of the Lizard Hotel.

Thus much I may say, that Mr. Johns in "A week at the Lizard," though he has fallen into sundry inaccuracies regarding other portions of the coast, is generally correct at Kynance; that is, after making due allowance for the change that is constantly being wrought on the softer portions of the rock by the unintermittent washing of the sea. And I cannot refrain from repeating here what I have elsewhere begged you to remember, that the beauties of Kynance lie in Mullyon and not "at the Lizard."

WRECKING AND SMUGGLING.

A WRITER in the October number of *Meliora* for 1865, in an article on "Cornwall and the Cornish," says, that in the last century, before the preaching of the Wesleys (who, as a certain witty cleric has observed, taught west country folk to "alter" their sins), "If a Cornishman said his prayers at all he would pray for a good wreck, and he would not scruple, by false signals and other means, to bring about such a catastrophe. And as to smuggling, that was considered a virtue. The revenue officers were esteemed public enemies. When Lord Exmouth's brother, Capt. Pellew, was sent to Falmouth to put down smuggling, he found some of his own officers running a contraband cargo of wine, in broad daylight, and in open port. One noted smuggler built himself a fortress, and armed it with long range guns, and one day when Capt. Pellew approached the stronghold more closely than was agreeable to its occupant, the fort opened fire upon the ship, and a sharp engagement followed, in which the aggressor happily was worsted."

On the 4th April 1786, the *Happy-go-lucky*, an armed lugger of 14 guns, commanded by a notorious smuggler, Welland, a Dover man, was surprised at anchor off Mullyon, by the revenue cutters *Hawk* and *Lark*, and captured after a chase to the westward, and a desperate fight, in which Welland was killed.—*Osler's Life of Lord Exmouth*, p. 386.

That a coast like this of Mullyon, with all its natural facilities for carrying on contraband operations, should not have been a favourite locality for "making a run," is hardly credible; but that blood shedding was as frequent as in many other parts is not likely, partly by reason of the smugglers taking greater care to avoid the others as much as possible, and partly because the revenue men, owing to the smallness of their force, would often, as a matter of prudence, keep out of the way until " the business " was completed.

I think it a mistake to pre-suppose such an invariable desperateness of character in those who took part in smuggling transactions as one finds so commonly attributed to them. Many and many a smuggler was otherwise a good, quiet, harmless creature enough, and who probably thought that in assisting to " run " a cargo or two he was hurting nobody. That the amount of smuggling that was carried on has ever been exaggerated I do not think. During the last century, and the early part of this, it is said, that there was hardly a family in these parts that was not more or less concerned in the trade ; and men living may even now, so far from considering it a disgrace, be heard to speak proudly of the day when they were engaged " in the smuggling *service.*"

Intimidation by a show of front or force often prevented an actual skirmish, and of this the following story affords a double example : " Many years ago," writes the Rev. Francis Gregory, a former vicar of this parish, "a Mount's Bay boat, commanded by a man nick-named ' Billy of Praow,' ran ashore at Mullyon Cove with a cargo of French brandy. *The Hecate*, gun-brig, was then stationed in Mount's Bay, and suspecting what was going on, despatched a boat to take possession of the smuggler. The crew of the latter, being taken by surprise, made little or no resistance, and abandoned their prize. The country people, however, being informed of the fact, collected in large numbers, broke into the armoury of Volunteers or Militiamen, at Trenance, furnished themselves with weapons and ammunition, went down to the cliffs, and firing upon the captors from behind the rocks, compelled them in turn to relinquish their booty, and to return to their ship. Many of the most respectable persons in the parish engaged in this lawless enterprise, and though they were threatened with prosecution, the matter was hushed up."

At another time two brothers, residing at Trenance, were suddenly aroused in the middle of the night, and called upon to assist in landing a cargo. One of them, either in a fit of nervousness, or from unwillingness to engage in the hazardous undertaking, found himself powerless to get on his clothing, and so retired to bed again. The other, and he who called him, were both drowned whilst engaged in their expedition.

Another story runs thus: A Mullyon man who had often crossed the channel and back in the capacity of *spotsman* (that is, one who has charge of the cargo, and determines the precise spot on the coast where it is to be landed), and who was known to have made many successful trips, was engaged on another; but on this occasion, the preventive men getting wind of his departure for France, determined to use every effort towards capturing him on his return, and to this end the revenue cutter was employed for some time in cruising off the Mullyon coast, while the land force was augmented by relays from far and near. He had employed a Mount's Bay boat for his voyage, and one fine evening, spite of the strict look-out that was being kept, he quietly landed his cargo of kegs at the foot of the cliffs, at a spot called *The Chair*, between Mullyon Cove and Predannack Head. He then sent off the boat with two hands, while he himself, and another of his men, went to meet their "friends" at Predannack, whom they found in the act of lighting a large fire, the common signal employed in such cases, to warn him of the presence and vigilance of "the enemy." To their astonishment he told them that "Cousin Jacky," which was the slang for "the Cognac," was, so far, safe on the rocks at the Chair. No time was then lost by the party in repairing thither, and on their arrival, so quietly was everything done, that they actually heard the thump of the bow of the revenue cutter's gig as she ran into their own retreating and empty boat. As quickly as possible they laid hold of and carried away as many kegs as they were able, depositing them, *pro tem*, in the adit of a deserted mine shaft, leaving the remainder on the rocks to take their chance. Meanwhile, the preventive gig had carried off the smuggler boat, and, taking the two men on board, made her fast to the cutter, and then returned to the cliffs to search for the precious cargo; but in vain; although the gig's men had actually landed within a hundred yards of the remaining kegs, they were not sufficiently wide awake to discover them, and so they pulled back to the cutter for the night after a fruitless errand. The smuggling party now returned to the Chair and shouldered all but two of the remaining kegs, these

last having somehow broken from their moorings ; and while they were taking
the others up over the cliff, the morning had sufficiently broken to enable
them to see the revenue cutter lying off in the roads at anchor, with their own
boat made fast to her astern.   Information was then forwarded to other
"friends" in Church town to the effect, that, although almost the whole cargo
had been safely landed, there were yet two casks that might be recovered.
Whereupon a fishing boat was sent out from the Cove, which, under the pre-
text of "whiffing," slowly passed down along under the Chair, and in a very
short time had the rest of "Cousin Jack" on board.   They had hardly got the
two kegs comfortably stowed, when by came the Revenue cutter's gig again, this
time engaged in "creeping" or dragging the bottom, in the hope of lighting
upon some portion of the suspected cargo.   The fishermen's whole attention
was of course absorbed in their fishing.   "What luck, lads?" cried one of the
coast guard, "What luck?"   "Why fish is very slight this mornin', very
slight," was the reply, and, with a sort of malicious self-satisfaction, was
added, "but we don't seem to be doin' so bad, neither."

Not many hours after, the original spotsman (the whole of his smuggled
cargo being by this time "safe") found his way once more to the cliffs, and
falling in with some of the supernumerary coast guard force, who had been
brought thither for the express purpose of taking him *flagrante delicto*, quoth
he, "You may go home again now boys, if you mind to, I won't keep 'ee
here no longer."

The said spotsman was not, however, always so fortunate.   On one occasion
he was shot by one of his own people.   This was by a mistake, of course.
He had come upon him suddenly in the dark and failed to immediately
respond to the challenge, whereupon the other fired at what he supposed to
be one of "the enemy."   It resulted only in the loss of a thumb.

They seem to have managed things in a very comfortable way in those
times.   Seldom any punishment is mentioned upon detection saving the com-
pulsory loss of the goods.   Four men were once thus caught by the captain
of a revenue cutter, with their boat full of tubs of contraband spirit.   One of
the men cried so bitterly, imploring the Captain not to rob him of what he
had paid for, begging him to restore some of it for the sake of his wife and

children, that the Captain took pity on him, and allowed him to carry off three of the kegs. When they reached the shore, and others were consulting how they might best divide the three tubs between four men, "Stop a bit," says Joe, "'Tis none of it yours, my dears, 'tis all mine. You didn't cry none any ef 'ee. The captain gave it to me for crying."

Another time, a boat's crew of four were ordered along-side the cutter, in Mount's Bay, and the captain discovering they had contraband with them, remarked to the younger of the party, "You, my fine fellow, will do for a man-of-war, and you three," addressing the others, "will go to prison." "All right, sir," replied one of them, "I've been in more French prisons than you've been in parish churches, I'll wage."

I have alluded to the fact that wrecking and smuggling were all but universal among the inhabitants. The writer in *Meliora* would have us believe that the former was practised by everybody, without exception. "It is related," he says, "that a Cornish clergyman found himself one Sunday morning being suddenly deserted by his congregation in the middle of his sermon, and that on ascertaining the cause to be news of a wreck, he cried out to his retreating flock to give him time only to divest himself of his robes that they might *all* start fair." And as to smuggling, another writer in *Household Words* observes, so universal in some parts was the interest in this lawless pursuit, that if the parson did not *always* hold the lantern on the rock during a landing, he was about the only man in the parish who had not some share in almost every venture.

But it is possible to paint the blackest too black. And as to the Preventive Service, at the time of which I write, when the whole force from Porthleven to the Lizard consisted of one officer and six men—what was it probable so small a force could effect against the mass of the population? Sometimes the preventive men were themselves prevented—now by the hospitality of the natives—and many is the "run" that has been made while officer and men have been busily engaged in discussing the good cheer of which they had been judiciously invited to partake —and now by the application of a persuasive force such as that which happened to an old and well-known coastguard's man who was gently bound hands and feet together and carefully deposited in a ditch while the smugglers' men were engaged in their lawless proceedings.

There is a strange wild spot near Mullyon Cove called the Vro Sand, at which place the coastguard officer then stationed at Mullyon—Lieutenant Drew—had reason to suppose that on a certain night an attempt would be made to ensure a successful "run." The weather was favourable as far as wind and sea were concerned, and mother moon being out of sight, the night was as dark as pitch. As the Lieutenant, accompanied by one of his men, was carefully watching the suspected spot, he suddenly came upon a party of smugglers awaiting the arrival of their vessel. On the sudden approach of the coastguard the men dispersed into the darkness, discharging a random shot or two by way of a welcome.

Escaping this danger (although one shot came so unpleasantly close as to whistle past between Lieutenant Drew and the coastguards-man at his side), they descended the cliff, and after a short inspection of the sandy cove, discovered a rope suspiciously attached to a rock and running out into the sea. If there had been any doubt before of the meaning of the armed party on the top of the cliff, there could be none now. The preventive men naturally began to haul in the line, and soon appeared a tub of spirits attached, then another and another until no less than a hundred were drawn to shore. And now rockets were sent up and pistols fired to summon the remainder of the coastguard force, and answering shots soon announced the arrival of the several patrols

One of the smuggling party had not gone off with the others, and this was none other than "the spotsman," a well-known inhabitant of Mullyon, and who had made many a successful voyage before. Perhaps he had concluded, like Will Watch, that this should be his last, not doubting but that his usual luck would attend him ; but he was to be disappointed as well as to have his courage severely tried. He narrowly escaped detection as the Lieutenant and his man were on their way down the cliff, for the coastguards-man's little dog had found him and would have, doubtless, given tongue, and told a tale, if he had not quickly and judiciously caressed the creature. And now, with the momentary chance of being discovered, he had the mortification of watching

from behind a rock the capture of his cargo for which he had risked so much
—the hauling in of keg after keg,—the assembling of the coastguard force,
and, whilst he dared not stir one foot himself nor utter a sound, of hearing their
congratulations one to another, and possibly of seeing the chalking of the
broad arrow on each of his cherished tubs.   Soon after, however, he managed
to elude observation, crept up the cliff and proceeded on his homeward way
                    " Unfriended, melancholy, slow."
Some of his companions, however, previous to the discovery, had managed to
secure a portion of the goods.   Crowds had collected on the following morning on the top of the cliff to witness the labour of hauling up the tubs ; and a
solemn silence reigned among them while the coastguards-men, as if perform-
ing mystic ceremonies, struggled to and fro and up the rocky gorge bending
beneath the weight of their spirituous burdens.   Among the spectators the
smuggling interest was well represented—they had come to take "a last, a
long, and sad farewell" of the precious kegs so shortly to be consigned to the
dark recesses of the Gweek Custom House.

It must have been a time of brisk trade for Mullyon when two landings were
attempted in the course of a fortnight.   At the first of these, as we have seen,
the smugglers fled on the approach of the coastguard, leaving their goods to
their fate ; and, at the next, two preventive men finding themselves in the
midst of a run, seized each man another with his burden, while a third smuggler drop'd his load and fled.   So that the capture this time consisted of two
men and six tubs.

A former chief boatman of coastguard, once stationed at Mullyon, Mr.
Williams, has informed me that he has had as many as 800 tubs of contraband
spirit in his charge at one time. *

At the last known attempt to effect a landing on the Mullyon coast Lieut.
Drew and a party of his men were on guard one night on Angrowse cliffs, when
they came upon a party who had settled themselves snugly behind a hedge.
No satisfactory replies being forthcoming to the challenge of the coastguard,

---

* For an interesting account of the capture of a single smuggler by this same Coastguards-man, see Hon.
Grantley Berkely's " *My Life and Recollections,*" *Vol.* 1.   The smuggler was engaged at about 2 o'clock, on
a moonless tho' starlight night, in hauling up some sunken kegs, about three miles from shore, when this
officer, by steadily sweeping the bay with his glass, and assisted by the reflection on the water of one bright star
only, eventually "spotted" his man, and then quietly awaited his return to the beach.

an order was given to search their persons, and as the search was proceeding the whole country round was suddenly illuminated with one great flash of light. The expected vessel had received her warning and made off, having dropt her cargo overboard. This was afterwards "crept" up by the Mullyon preventive men, assisted by the crew of the Penzance Revenue Cutters.

So ended the last recorded smuggling transaction between Mullyon and the French port of Roscoff.

Many of the houses in Mullyon have still, though they have long ceased to be used for such purposes, cupboards with false backs and bottoms, secret shafts alongside of the staircases, small chambers in the thicknesses of the walls, or wells underneath a double flooring, wherein contraband goods were wont to be deposited.

Of "wrecking" proper, by which I mean alluring a ship to her destruction, many is the day since such villany has been resorted to, but of the more moderate form of wrecking—that of appropriating to oneself whatsoever bit of flotsam or jetsam one comes across, or even of stripping off portions of a partially broken hull, this is not so rare now when an opportunity offers itself.

"A century ago," says Cyrus Redding, "in the superstitious days when, according to vulgar belief, the clergyman of the parish had his familiar spirit, the plunder of wrecks might have been made a charge with greater justice, but the very rumour now that any man had been guilty of such atrocity, would expel him from society in Cornwall, and from the county itself."

Our shores are now too well guarded for much plunder of this nature to be committed, as I have heard it said more than once "The coastguards-men and the police are the only persons who stand a chance of picking up anything worth anything after a wreck." That a wreck, especially if no lives be lost, is still looked upon as a sort of God-send to the neighbourhood, is evident from the amount of envy and jealousy which shews itself in those who do not happen to reside in the immediate vicinity, as Pope sings :—

> "Then full against his Cornish lands they roar,
> And two rich shipwrecks bless the lucky shore."

When the "*North Britain*" went on shore near the Mount, in Dec., 1868, I heard it remarked in Mullyon "Pity she went so far into the bay. What do

they in to Penzance want of a wreck in there? If she'd come in here she
might have done some good!" Feelings of this nature are not, I apprehend,
confined to these parts. There is, after all, a good deal of human nature, as
Artemus Ward remarks, about mankind in general.

Instances, however, are not wanting to shew that while the dwellers on our
coasts would not scruple to appropriate portions of wrecked timber and the
like, no kind of dishonesty is felt or intended. After the wreck of the *Jonkheer*,
detailed below, some fishermen—Jackson and Jones, from Penberth Cove, on
the opposite side of the bay, while employed in fishing up blocks of tin which
had formed part of the ship's cargo, found, among other things, a small box
containing coins and bank notes, to the value of £1,000 and upwards. They
immediately brought the box and its contents ashore and handed them up to
the authorities, who, I must say, did not display a great amount of wisdom on
the circumstance. The men claimed, and afterwards received, their salvage
portion of course, but from the time they brought the box on shore, though
not before, as long as they were engaged in their work at the sunken wreck,
they were accompanied by a coastguards-man whenever they went afloat—
were placed under strict supervision as a reward for their honesty! Such
shortsighted policy is not calculated to render the coastguard popular among
those who still look upon them with a certain amount of dislike. Such a
course of action is no incentive to honest dealing, but rather the contrary.

WRECKS.

LIST OF WRECKS.

Date.	NAMES.	Locality.	Drowned.	Buried at Mullyon.
1803. July...	No account of wreck			1
1809. Jan....	No account of wreck			8
1809. Nov....	Barque, "Cunningham"	Polurrian		
1810. Aug...	No account of wreck			10
1815. July...	Dutch Barque	The Vraddan...		
1817. Jan. 7	French brig, "L'Hammican" ...	Gunwalloe	13	3
1832. Aug...	Barque	The Rill.........		
1833. Feb....	Smack	Vounder Nean.		
1833. Oct....	Smack	Vraddan		
1838. June 20	"Neapolitan"	Carrag lûz	15	11
1839. Apr. 22	"Penrice Castle" and 2 others	Polurrian		
1839. Aug....	Brigantine	Kynance	5	
1840. June...	Smack	The Vraddan...	1	1

Date.	NAMES.	Locality.	Drowned.	Buried at Mullyon.
1847. Oct. 11	Finland barque, "Iris"............	Poljew	6	
1858. Sept. 17	"Glencoe" and "Mary".........	Polurrian	1	1
1858. Sept. 22	"Chester"..........................	At sea		
1862. Jan. 11	"Dollard"..........................	The Rill........	6	1
1862. Jan. 22	"Padre"	Poljew	13	1
1862. Dec. 12	"Arwenack".......................	Deserted	5	1
1865. April 17	"John Mc'Intyre"	Gue Greze......		
1867. Jan. 6	"Margaret," "Cherub," and "Ebbw Vale" .... }	Meres Ledges..	4	3
1867. Mar. 26	"Jonkheer"	Mên y Grib ...	24	15
1867. Oct. 22	"Achilles"	Polurrian		
1868. Jan. 21	"Maria Louisa"	Mullyon Island.	3	
1869. Feb. 9	"Calcutta's" boat................	(?) Mullyon Isld.	21	4
1869. April 22	"Remedy"	Predannack Hd		
1871. Jan. 27	French brig, "Berthe & Leontiné"	Deserted		
1873. Mar. 1	"Boyne"	Meres Ledges...	15	7
1874. Dec. 8	"Diana"	Church Cove...		

It will be remarked that out of all these not one vessel that ever touched the shore got off again, save the *John Mc'Intyre*, and she was of set purpose thrust in, and was floated again under very favourably exceptional circumstances.

In July, 1815, a Dutch barque, laden with a cargo of tea, came in during a thick fog so near the cliffs that the crew deserted her, most of them leaving in the ship's boat, and so came on shore. The vessel, striking on the Vraddan, went to pieces, and the shores were soon covered with the scattered cargo. Hence, she is commonly spoken of as "the tea wreck."

1832. A barque came on shore between Kynance Cove and the Rill, laden with coffee. So known as "the coffee wreck."

1833. February. A smack becoming embayed, the captain beached her to save life. She came on shore at Porth Pyg, under Vounder Nean, stood nearly whole for several days, and then broke up.

1833. October. A smack belonging to Padstow, laden with coals, "The Bellamy," struck on the Vraddan, and then came on to the Vro Cove. There she lay during several tides, while unsuccessful attempts were made to get her off. She went to pieces. All hands saved.

1838. June 30. A Neapolitan barque, of slender build, of about 300 tons, with a cargo of salt, came in during the night under Carrag Lûz, on the southern part of Polurrian. The wind had been blowing a strong gale from S.S.W., and a thick fog had prevailed all the preceding day, and through the night. The first sign of a wreck was the discovery, in the early morning, by a couple of our villagers, that Polurrian Cove was one mass of wreckage. All on board had perished, and this is therefore known among us as "the dead wreck." All hands (supposed to have been 15) drowned. 11 of these were buried in Mullyon churchyard.

1839. April 22. Three small vessels were discovered under Henscath, or between that and the Flag-staff. The *Penrice Castle*, of Port Talbot, laden with coal, Capt. Macnamara, and two other brigantines, laden with slate. One of these last ran into the *Penrice Castle*, which vessel came ashore at Pedn y Ké, the other under Carrag Lûz, and the third struck on the rocks at Polglâs, under Merres Hedge. All three soon went to pieces. No lives lost.

1839. August 1. With an E.S.E. breeze a brigantine was lying to just inside the Lizard Head, when the wind suddenly veered round to S.W., and brought her on shore at Par-an-heol, between Kynance Cove and the Rill. Supposed cargo, salt. All hands, 5, drowned.

1840. (?) June. A smack struck on the Vraddan, and went down. One man washed off and drowned, and on September 17, the body of a man was found at Pedny Ké, in a very decomposed state ; had been in the water many weeks.

1847. October 11. A Finland barque, the *Iris*, Captain Kyllen, laden with wheat, came in during the night on Kinsale Rock, Poljew. Part of the crew climbed up the rock by sticking their knives into the interstices, there remaining till the tide had ebbed sufficiently to allow them to gain terra firma. The vessel shortly broke up—6 drowned, and 6 saved.

1857. August. Richard George and Frank Harris, two Mullyon fishermen, were out looking after their crab-pots, off Pigeon Hugo, in foggy weather, when they observed a very large vessel, with studding sails set, running in before a light S.S.W. wind, right in the direction of the cliffs. She passed their boat, and shortly came to a dead stand, a little further in. Henry George and Samuel Hitchens, two other Mullyon fishermen, were, at this time, in their crabbing-boat, at moorings, just off Vellan Head, and, hearing a gun fire, made for the spot whence the report proceeded, soon falling in with the vessel. S. Hitchens was taken on board. She proved to be *H.M.S. Exmouth.* "Where are we ?" demanded the Captain. Hitchens told him, and advised what was to be done, but then, there she lay, with Pengersick point on her starboard bow, for a couple of hours, bumping on the sand. Auxiliary steam having been meanwhile got up, Hitchens piloted the ship out of danger, and then, having received a certificate of the service he had rendered, left again in his own boat.

Three months elapsed, and as he had heard of nothing in the shape of remuneration, he thought it would be as well to remind the authorities of the circumstance ; so, after consultation with the coastguard-officer, he had to appear before the Inspecting-Commander, to relate his story and produce his certificate. Eventually he received £5 (!) as a reward for having extricated one of Her Majesty's ships of war from a position of very great danger.

She left her anchor and 15 fathoms of chain behind her, together with a portion of her false keel and copper sheathing. So close indeed had she lain to the cliff that any one of the crew might have jumped off her spanker boom on to the rocks.

WRECKS OF THE "GLENCOE" AND THE "MARY."

A number of wind-bound vessels were lying at anchor in Mullyon Roads on 17th September, 1858, when the wind, which had been for some time easterly, suddenly shifted and soon blew a gale on to the land. Many of these vessels hardly escaped being embayed, but all save two manged to weather the Lizard. One of these, a brig, named the "Glencoe," of Whitby, was observed by the coastguard and others on the cliffs, about 3 o'clock in the afternoon, to be dragging her anchor, and before long she was stranded amid the breakers on Polurrian sands ; and as wave after wave broke clean over her, the hull being almost completely enveloped in the surf, the crew betook themselves to the rigging.

The Rocket Apparatus for the establishment of a communication between a stranded vessel and the shore was at that time unknown at Mullyon, and in this emergency it occurred to Lieut. Drew, of the coastguard, that it might be possible to fire a light fishing-line across to the wreck by means of an ordinary signal rocket ; but the attempt was unsuccessful, by reason of the distance of the vessel from the shore. The coastguard's boat was then sent for by land with the idea that in her it might be possible, later in the afternoon, to reach the vessel, as from the position in which she was lying, she acted as a kind of breakwater ; moreover, the tide was on the ebb, and there was every hope of rescuing the crew if the vessel held together long enough.

In the dusk of the evening it was discovered that the other vessel was gradually nearing the cliff, on the northern side of the sandy beach. The majority of the spectators now made a rush in the direction of this vessel, and the shrieks from the crew of the brig, who fancied themselves thus deserted, were heard above the storm. It was first thought when this vessel, the "Mary," of Bridgwater, struck the rocks on Polbream Point, that she was deserted, as no one could be seen on board. She had parted her chain cable near the anchor, and came in dragging the remaining chain along the bottom. Soon

H

after she struck, the men emerged from below, and as she was nearer the low cliff than the *Glencoe* was to the shore, a line was, after one unsuccessful effort, thrown across her by means of a signal-rocket. A larger rope was then attached and was being haul'd out, when the shore end slipped, and would have escaped altogether had not a Mullyon man, John Mundy, dashed into the waves at the risk of his life and recovered it. A temporary sling of rope was then constructed by Mr. Williams, chief boatman, coastguard, and in it one of the crew was safely hauled on shore ; a second man, the captain, was next brought in ; but the third, a large, heavily-built man, when about half way between the vessel and the cliff, lost his hold on the ropes and fell. In falling, however, his feet became entangled in the sling, which presently so twisted itself around the warp, that it could not be moved either backwards or forwards ; and there the poor fellow hung suspended by one leg, now hoisted high, mid-air, now dipped into the foaming water beneath, as the vessel rolled from one side to another and alternately tightened and slackened the warp. " Haul the man in ! " cries Mr. Williams, " Haul ! you can but pull the life out of him ; he'll be killed there if he isn't dead already " ; and with a long pull and a strong pull of many hands, they haul'd the poor body in—battered and bruised to be sure, but still alive ! With every care, he was tenderly carried to the Old Inn, where, happily, it was found that no bones were broken. He had, most fortunately, not struck the rocks in either of his rapid descents.

There were no others left on board but one poor boy, whom the crew had in vain tried to persuade to precede them. As this last came in, he was to be descried in the dim twilight still clinging to one of the masts. Another sling was quickly rigged up and sent out to him, but he still refused, from fright, doubtless, to move ; then with a sudden crash and a swirl the masts fell over, the vessel broke up, and the poor lad, calling piteously on his mother, was en-gulphed amid the roar of the waters. His body was afterwards recovered and buried in Mullyon churchyard, Sept. 20th. The crew did not know his name or place of abode, he had only joined them a week before at Bridgwater, and went by the name of Frederick.

All this time the poor fellows on board the *Glencoe* were still in her rigging, doubtful whether they should escape with their lives ; while the sea had been breaking over them for hours, and there seemed no prospect of relief. The vessel had lifted in a little towards the northern part of the beach, and, one signal rocket remaining, it was fired just about the time of low water, but this also fell short. The crew then supposing the tide had turned, and fearing the vessel would break up with its return, determined upon a desperate effort. One of them, with a line lashed round him, jumped overboard in the hopes of taking it on shore. They had taken the precaution to have a second line attached to him, so that in case of failure, they might haul him on board again ; but the brave fellow, by dint of great energy and determination, approached the beach, while the men there formed a chain of hands, and venturing out into the surf, secured him and his line, just as he was becoming entangled in the wreckage of the other vessel. Communication being thus established, all the crew came on shore in safety, though sadly benumbed and exhausted by their eight hours exposure to wind and waves, between 12 and 1 at night.

Part of the cargo of coal was saved; the damaged hull remained on the beach for some time, and gradually broke, or was broken, up.

FOUNDERING OF THE " CHESTER."

On the night of the 22nd of the same month, two coastguard men—Cotton and Sterling—observed a boat, with four hands on board, making in for Mullyon Cove. Knowing the danger the boat would be exposed to in the heavy surf that was then breaking on the beach, they beckoned them off the shore, and caused them to understand that they were to wait for a signal from them to attempt a landing. The rule with us is to wait outside the surf until we see "the third big wave" break on Treguin (a rock on the northern point of Mullyon island,) and then "to pull for dear life" and come in on the back of the breaker ; and, so these poor fellows, following the signalled instructions of the coastguard, came in. As they jumped on to the shingle "That's all right" cried one of them. We'll hope he meant the same as two of his comrades, who fell on their knees and returned their silent thanks to the Almighty for their deliverance. They reported that their vessel, a schooner, called the *Chester*, Capt. F. Miners, of Plymouth, had been caught

by the storm in the bay, and having carried away her canvas, had become unmanageable.   That she had foundered on the Boa Shoal, a sand-bank to the
southward of Mullyon island, and that they had only time to escape in their
boat when they saw the vessel go down.   On the Saturday following, sails,
spars, rigging, &c., were found floating in a large mass, and were warped on
shore.

WRECK OF THE " DOLLARD."

On the 11th January, 1862, at 7.30 a.m., the Dutch brig the *Dollard*, laden
with wheat, from Trieste for Falmouth, struck on the cliffs near The Rill, at a
spot called by fishermen " The Pound."   One of the crew saved himself by
jumping on to a rock and clambering the cliff, whence he made his way to
Kynance Farm.   The captain, his son, and four seamen perished, and the
vessel went to pieces in ten minutes.   Near the place where she struck is a
a cave or "ogo," the access to which is so low that it rarely opens sufficiently
to allow the passage of a boat.   But about a month after this wreck, some
fishermen, in very still weather, effected an entrance into the cave, the bottom
of which is always filled with water, and there they found portions of the
masts and spars of the unfortunate *Dollard*, which had been knocking about
in this subterranean chaldron ever since she broke up.   Only one of the bodies
of the six drowned men was recovered, and this was buried in Mullyon
churchyard.

WRECK OF THE " PADRE."

On the 22nd January, 1862, the Austrian barque *Padre*, 400 tons, Captain
Andrea Bogdanovich, with a cargo of wheat, from Trieste, in a gale from S.S.W.,
was blown on to the rocks at Poljew, at 6.30 a.m.   The captain, his bride, an
infant, and 10 of the crew perished, and the vessel went to pieces immediately.
Four men, Italians, were saved.   They first reached Kinsale Rock.
Thence two men were rescued by Goldsack, a coastguard's-man, allowing himself to be lowered over cliff by a rope, and so securing his men ; another was
caught by another coastguard's-man, by means of a boat hook ; and the fourth
was saved by Henry George, a Mullyon fisherman.   Had they remained on
Kinsale Rock until the tide had ebbed, they might all have walked on shore ;

but of this, they could not possibly have been aware.   Goldsack and George received the Humane Society's medal for their heroic conduct.

13 persons were drowned at this wreck, and the body of the child only was recovered and buried in Mullyon.

On the day of the sale of the timber, &c., from the wreck of the *Padre*, the whole of Poljew beach was thickly lined with persons of all classes, who had assembled, either as intending purchasers at, or witnesses of the sale.   Suddenly, at about half flood, and without any kind of warning, a huge tidal wave came sweeping up the length and breadth of the Cove, carrying all before it, masts, spars, piles of broken timber, stores and other portions of the wreck, and most of the people as well.   A horse and cart were capsized and drawn along for some distance, and two men found themselves transported up as far as the bridge.   No further damage was done beyond the numerous wettings and the bruises that accrued to some of the less fortunate ones.   One old lady was, however, taken out seaward, but was happily arrested by a mass of wreckage and brought safely ashore again on the return wave.

WRECK OF THE "ARWENACK."

On Friday, 12th December, 1862, the *Arwenack*, of Truro, with a cargo of copper-ore from Devoran, for South Wales, lost her sails in Mount's Bay during a gale from S.S.W.   The men, five in number, taking to the boat, were capsized and drowned off Polurrian.   This occurred during the night.   The vessel herself was washed in to Gunwalloe Cove, where she broke up.   Her sails, &c., were brought in to Mullyon Cove on the following Sunday morning.

5 hands drowned, 1 buried in Mullyon churchyard.

ROCKET APPARATUS.

After the wreck of the *Padre*, mention was made on the back of the Coast guard Casualty Report to the Board of Trade, of the great need of rocket-apparatus for this station, and subsequent events have shewn, not only how great was the need, but also how very great has been the value of that simple invention.   Lord, then Mr. Robartes, on hearing of the report, sent his steward to make enquiries whether a lifeboat would not prove equally beneficial ; but the reply returned from the parish then was, that " a lifeboat would

be useless, unless the rocks at the entrance of the Cove were cleared out."
A Mansbury's rocket apparatus, with its car, was therefore sent to Mullyon
station in the year 1862, and it has since been the means of saving at least 30
lives.

THE " JOHN MC'INTYRE."

On the 17th April, 1865, the *John Mc'Intyre*, a large screw steamer, an iron
boat, bound for S. Wales, struck, in a fog, slightly, as it was thought, on a rock
off the Lizard, and the captain not apprehending danger, did not wait to over-
haul. It was soon evident, however, that she had sprung a considerable leak,
as a quantity of water had found its way into her in a very short time. The
captain, knowing the coast, then determined to beach his vessel on one of the
sandy coves under Mullyon, but before he could execute his idea, the water
was gaining upon her so rapidly, that he was compelled, although the weather
was far from foul, to act promptly ; he, with a boldness which deserved success,
therefore turned her, at full speed, into the narrow cleft in the cliffs at Gue
Greze. As she rushed in and partly up the little beach, she split a rock
asunder as if it had been clay, and there she lay comfortably " shored up."

Some weeks elapsed before the attempts to float her again were successful,
during which time the weather, fortunately, continued fair, and the wind off
shore, and eventually, partly by stopping the leak with bags full of clay, and
partly with empty tar barrels, the water being pumped out of her, she was
again brought to float, and in that state was towed over the bay to Penzance,
where her damages were temporarily patched previous to her going into dry
dock elsewhere.

All on board had, of course, been landed in safety when she first came in,
and all articles of value were at the same time secured.

WRECKS OF THE " CHERUB," THE " MARGARET," AND THE " EBBW VALE."

The storm which visited Mount's Bay on the night of Friday, 4th January,
1867, and throughout the following day, was one of the severest which had
been experienced on this coast for a number of years. It commenced by
blowing hard from the eastward, and so prevented a large number of coasting
vessels from weathering the Lizard. These, as is commonly the case under

such circumstances, had come to anchor in Mullyon roads, the only anchorage
that is at all safe in the neighbourhood, but at the same time, one which is
always to be used with caution, as the wind often makes a sudden shift to S.
or S.W., and thereby renders the position of such vessels one of imminent
peril. This was the case on the evening of the 5th January, and towards midnight, it was blowing a whole gale from S.W. Many of the vessels had
weighed or slipped their anchors, and got out of the bay ; but two of them,
the *Cherub*, of Swansea, and the *Margaret*, of Teignmouth, in an attempt to
escape, had come into collision, one man, George Mudge, belonging to the
Margaret, getting on board the *Cherub* at the time. The *Margaret* again
dropped anchor, and those on board the *Cherub* finding her unmanageable,
and seeing she must be driven in against the cliffs, took to their boat, and by
good fortune, being carried in on the top of a breaker to the sandy beach at
Polurrian, and jumping out just as she took ground, landed themselves without
a bruise. They then groped their way about for some time, and at last
descried lights in the cottage windows at La Frowder, whence they were
accompanied by some of the fishermen to Church Town.

Daybreak on the following morning—Sunday, the Festival of the Epiphany
—discovered the shore and base of the cliffs strewn for miles with debris of
wreckage, but five vessels were still in the roads, all anchored within a mile of
the land, and therefore still in danger. The *Cherub* had, of course, disappeared, having broken up during the night. There was no lifeboat at Mullyon
then, so messengers were sent off to Porthleven, and the " Agar Robartes "
was got ready, and being drawn by six powerful horses, passed through the
streets of Helston just about the time that people were going to church. A large
number of Helston folk, hitherto ignorant of the scene on the coast, followed
the lifeboat, meanwhile, hundreds of the inhabitants of the neighbourhood of
Mullyon had assembled on the cliffs.

It was a glorious morning, the sun was shining in all his brightness, and a
light balmy breeze was coming in from the westward, but there was a tremendous sea still running, the effect of the long continued storm. And there
was the *Margaret*, rolling and pitching heavily, right under Angrowse cliffs, and
within a cable's length of them, with her four remaining hands on board.

Would the lifeboat arrive before she met her fate, for sooner or later, smashed she must be, as all on shore foresaw ? Her anchor was dragging, and the tide was on the ebb. The coastguards-men, with the rocket apparatus, had been on the ground since 7.30 in the morning, but at that time the vessel was out of reach of the rocket line. Several rockets had been fired, but all failed of falling over the vessel ; and some hours must elapse after the departure of the messenger, before the Porthleven lifeboat could be drawn over 12 miles of very hilly country to reach the spot. " Is there any gentleman who will go or send for the Lizard Lifeboat ?" asked the chief boatman of the coastguard (why she had not been sent for in the first case, is incomprehensible, excepting on the ground that Porthleven being the coastguard station, it seemed natural to look there for assistance.) Hardly were the words spoken, when Mr. J. B. Kempthorne (the Vicar had told his churchwarden there would be no service held in Church that morning, and therefore he was free to go) started off on horseback " bare ridge," as he was, for the Lizard. " Tell them not to wait to pick up their crew," shouted the coastguard, " Send the boat at once, we will man her ; " for at that time there was no lifeboat at Cadgwith as now, and part of the Lizard boat's crew resided there. It should be mentioned, however, as a fact, reflecting very great credit on the hon. secretary and the crew of the Lizard lifeboat, that within forty minutes of their receiving Mr. Kempthorne's message, the boat with her coxswain and crew were in Mullyon Church Town, having come round more than six miles from their boat house.

Still the doomed craft held on, heaving and pitching more heavily than ever, as the tide began to run more swiftly. Why the poor men on board made no kind of effort to save themselves, seemed a mystery. They could easily have established a communication with those on shore ; a barrel, a spar, an oar, anything that would float with a light line attached, would have drifted in before the wind, to the spot where several persons were standing on a ledge of rocks below the cliff; but although all kinds of signs and gestures were made by these and others (Geo. Mudge, their old shipmate, among the number,) they contented themselves by remaining with their arms folded over the bulwark of the vessel, as if, which seems incredible, unconscious of the danger they were in, or of the probable fate that awaited them. They did make one attempt by throwing a ladder over-board, on which they essayed to come ashore, but finding it would not float them all, they clambered back - into the vessel again, relying, it is supposed, for assistance, which could not yet be afforded them.   None but a lifeboat could possibly have lived in or worked her way out through the tremendous surf, and the anxiety of the assembled crowd was becoming intense, as eager eyes were cast now in direction of Poljew, now towards Polurrian in search of the expected aid.   It could not last like this very much longer, the water under the ship's bottom was getting shallower and shallower, and she still dragged.   Ah ! it's all over with her ; after a larger wave than usual, down she went, bumping her stern post on the hard rock beneath—her cable parted, she gave one plunge forward, heeled over and came broadside on, split open lengthways, and let out her cargo of coals, which blackened the water for a moment, —broke in two a-midships and disappeared, all this occupying scarcely more time than it has taken to detail it.   Then appeared an indescribable mass of broken spars, masts, and cordage, being tumbled about in the waves, and a piece of the stern with deck attached, and one man clinging to it.   The other three were seen no more.

This man crawled up to the uppermost part of this fragment of the wreck several times between the intervals of the breaking waves, but only to be hurled down again as each successive wave came on.   So close was he to those who had collected under cliff, that amid the thundering of the sea, they could hear him calling on them to throw him a line.   A line was thrown, and a rocket fired, but without success ; and to attempt to cross the boiling channel which separated them from him, would have been utter destruction.   In the interval, between two breakers, he let go his hold, ran along a short ridge of partially covered rock, and committed himself to the seething foam.   It was evident that the force of the sea had already half beaten the life out of him, and that he could not swim.   He struggled for a few moments amidst the broken spars and rigging that was washing about, and then sank !   " Alas ! poor fellow ! he's gone too !" murmured the crowd.   But no !   There he is again, carried out by the undercurrent some 30 yards to the left, still struggling for dear life. He sinks again.   " Dear soul ! how hard he fights !   He deserved to be saved too !   But he's gone now."   No ; again ; not yet !   He now appears at

I

the other end of the channel, and to the right of the spot where he first was, still living, still battling with the sea and the broken fragments of the wreck. He sinks once more, " It's all over with him now," and many began to turn from the sickening scene, when yet once more he appears, being carried back again by the return wave to the very spot where he was at first. " Fire him a line !" and the rocket is once again off on its would-be merciful errand. " He's caught it !" and a hand is raised above the water, grasping a line, as much as to say "I have it ! Haul in !". But alas, it was not *the* line—merely a bit of the vessel's cordage, which to him was useless. A huge wave followed, which lifted him head and shoulders out of water, when a recoil caught him and hurled him against the rocks. Two days after, a body was picked up about half a mile to the southward, with the skull broken in—it was that of the ill-fated captain of the *Margaret*, who had to-day, so long and yet so vainly, battled with the unsparing elements.

Of the other vessels, two, that were anchored further off from the shore, managed to get away during the morning ; but the fifth still lay at anchor, without a sign of life on board. It was concluded, as was afterwards proved to have been the case, that she had been deserted, her crew having been taken off by another vessel. She, too, broke her moorings, and coming ashore on Sunday evening, was soon, though iron built, pounded to bits on the very spot where the *Margaret* was wrecked, and where the *Cherub* had broken up on the previous morning and night. She proved to have been the *Ebbw Vale*, of Swansea.

Returning to Mullyon Church Town, we found there both the lifeboats that had been summoned. They had arrived only just in time to be told that they were too late.

" Something must be done," was the general feeling, " to prevent the recurrence of so sad a catastrophe," and the expression of this feeling found vent in the public meeting that ensued.

PUBLIC MEETING AT MULLYON.

On Monday the 14th of January, 1867, a meeting of the parishioners of Mullyon, convened by the Vicar, was held, for the purpose of considering, in reference to the recent wrecks and loss of life in the immediate neighbourhood, the necessity of endeavouring at once to secure a lifeboat to be stationed at Mullyon. In spite of the extreme severity of the weather, the meeting was well attended by the farmers and fishermen of the parish, and the following resolutions were unanimously carried as expressive of the opinion of those assembled.

1. "That in consequence of the numerous wrecks that occur upon the immediate coast, it is incumbent upon the inhabitants of the neighbourhood to adopt some more efficient means than have hitherto been available for the preservation of life and property."

2. "That as Mullyon Roads is the only anchorage in Mount's Bay for vessels bound eastwards during the prevalence of easterly winds, yet as vessels so seeking shelter there are, nevertheless, liable to be placed in imminent danger by reason of a sudden shift of wind to the S. or S.W. (an occurrence far from infrequent), the best, if not the only, effectual relief in such cases would be by means of a lifeboat stationed at Mullyon."

3. "That it is equally desirable that a simultaneous effort be made, either by application to Government, or by other means, to form a harbour of refuge at Mullyon Cove by filling up what is termed "The Gap"—the narrow shallow channel between the Island and the main—or by placing a floating breakwater there."

The following facts were elicited in the course of the meeting from the mouths of residents, coastguards, fishermen, and crabbers : That, had the stretch of water inside the island and between it and the cove been so protected, there would then exist a harbour into which all the vessels recently wrecked in Mount's Bay might have run with safety. That it is hardly a rare occurrence for as many as two hundred sail to be seen at anchor in Mullyon Roads waiting for "a start," and that many of these are often caught by a sudden change of wind. That if so caught, as things are at present, there can be little hope for the lives of their crews. That on this part of the coast so violent are the storms, and so great their force, that a vessel commonly goes to pieces within ten minutes of her striking the rocks ; and but little, if anything, can be done for the crew when once she gets into the surf. That of all spots in Mount's Bay, Mullyon is that which most needs a lifeboat.

The meeting terminated by requesting the undernamed gentlemen to form a committee for the purpose of carrying into effect its resolutions : The Vicar, Rev. E. G. Harvey; Mr. J. B. Kempthorne, Polhormon ; Mr. William Nicholas ; Mr. John Thomas, Predannack ; Mr. Joseph Thomas, Colroger ; Mr. Thomas Shepherd, Tremenhehe ; and Mr. Peter Williams, Angrowse.

This committee immediately put themselves into communication with the Royal National Life Boat Institution ; the result of which was an offer on the part of the Institution of a lifeboat which had been subscribed for by the Wesleyan Methodists, in memory of the Rev. Daniel J. Draper, who unfortunately perished on the occasion of the foundering of the *London*, in the Bay of Biscay, in the year 1866, and who was a native of Cornwall ; his friends being desirous that the lifeboat should be placed on that coast.

Lord Robartes, with his accustomed liberality, speedily granted the ground for the boat house, and also promised pecuniary assistance for the needs of the branch. Nothing then remained but to build the house and await the arrival of the boat.

" March 15, 1867. We have had between 400 and 500 vessels anchoring in our Roads during the last few days. All, I am glad to say, have got away safely ; but yesterday two large barques were in a very critical position for some hours. Had it come on to blow there would have been no chance of escape for them."

WRECK OF THE " JONKHEER MEESTER VAN DE WALL."

About 11 o'clock, on the evening of 25th March, 1867, the Vicar was sitting alone in his dining room, reading, the other members of the family having retired to rest, and, little heeding the storm without, was deeply engaged with the contents of the book before him. Suddenly he started to his feet. He heard, or fancied that he heard, a prolonged shrieking wail, as of many voices. Immediately unfastening the window shutters, and throwing up the sash, he listened long and anxiously. The wind, which was blowing a gale, swept right in from the sea, and its howling among the trees, together with the thundering of the surf upon the shore, distant hardly more than half mile from the vicarage, were all that could be heard. No cry ; no blue light, nor signal of distress. The Vicar closed the window, and concluding that the sound he had heard was nothing but the wailing of the storm, he retired for the night.

The following morning early he was aroused by tidings that a large vessel had gone ashore during the night, and that a number of persons had been drowned. The coastguards-man on watch had come up to the village about 3 o'clock, a.m., with the alarm that *he had seen a large barque dangerously near the cliffs*; so the rocket apparatus was at once got out and carried down to Poljew Cove (there was no life boat station at Mullyon then), on past Poljew towards Gunwalloe, but nothing was to be seen of any vessel. Meanwhile, some of the villagers had gone along the cliff tops between Polurrian and Poljew, and there they descried parts of a wreck ; and, at length, clambering about the rocks under cliff, the sole survivor of the unfortunate vessel's company, a Greek sailor. He was so bruised and benumbed, that at the moment, he could have given no very intelligible account of the wreck, even if the coast-guard could have understood the little English he was master of. Soon the stern of the vessel was found washed in between two ledges of rocks on the southern side of Poljew Cove, and near it the bodies of two females, with nothing but the remnants of their night dresses about them ; then the body of another female was discovered, and later in the day those of a sailor and an infant were picked up. These were all taken and laid in the tower of Mullyon Church to await a coroner's inquest.

About 9 o'clock, the Greek sailor having had a dry suit of clothes provided him, and some refreshment given him, the Vicar went to see what he could learn from him concerning the ship and her cargo, &c. The man seemed but little inclined to be communicative, and his ordinary language, a mixture of Greek and Italian, was difficult to be interpreted. He said he had joined the ship at Batavia, but he did not know her name nor the name of the captain ! He had slightly injured his right arm in clambering up the cliff, but beyond a few bruises, was otherwise uninjured. He had on him a lady's gold watch and chain which was difficult to account for in the case of a common sailor like himself. There were five and twenty souls on board at the time of the wreck, and this was the third time that he had been wrecked, being the only one saved on each occasion. The vessel must have sailed in right against the cliffs between Poljew and Polurrian, striking her keel on Mên y Grib rocks, having her back broken upon them, and then slipping out and subsiding in deeper water, with the exception of the stern portion, which was broken off and washed into Poljew. At the time she struck he said that he and two other sailors were forward on the jib-boom, all three sprang off it on to the face of the cliff, two being by the next wave sucked backed into the sea and drowned. He himself held on, managed to scale the cliff in the darkness, and then wandered about till he was found by the coast-guard and villagers. Of the women washed ashore one was the body of a large person, probably Dutch, and about fifty years of age, having nothing on at the time but two stockings, and these both on the left leg. This person proved afterwards to be S. W., of whom more anon.

She was a passenger from Batavia, in charge of a gentleman on board. Another, aged about 23, dark hair and finely formed features, with but drawers and stockings on, a gold clasp ring, and a gold heart-shaped black enamelled locket enclosing miniature photograph of a young gentleman. She was found to be J. B., fiancée of Herr M., of Utrecht, to whom she was shortly to be married. The third, a short, bright haired young woman, S. G., who passed on board for the Captain's wife. She had been confined on board about three weeks previously; and the drowned infant was her child. It had on, when picked up, its little night-dress and cap, and a coral necklace.

This was all the information that the sailor was able or willing to afford.

Along the shores coffee in the berry was washing in in very large quantities, as the waves completed their destruction of the ship, and piles of sugar baskets—tubular affairs, 6 feet long by two feet in diameter, composed of split bamboo, bound with cane, and lined with dry leaves—were to be seen lying about at the waters edge in every direction.

The inquest was held on Wednesday, at the Old Inn, by Mr. Roscorla, county coroner. The Greek sailor was examined through Giacomo Carlo Balestreri, of Penzance, interpreter. He said, "my name is Georgio Buffani ; I was seaman on board the ship which belonged to Dordrecht. I joined the

WRECK OF THE "JONKHEER."

From a water-colour painting by the Rev. F. C. Jackson, now in possession of Walter J. Goldsmith, Esq.

ship at Batavia, but I do not know the name of the ship, or the name of the Captain." On his being shewn, however, the official list of Dutch East India-men, he pointed to one built 1854, the *Kosmopoliet*, Captain König. "We sailed," said he, "from Batavia for Rotterdam on 25th November last, with a cargo of coffee, spice, and sugar, there was a quantity of tin also on board as ballast. The vessel's crew consisted of 20 men, all told, and there were 6 passengers, viz., 3 ladies, 2 gentlemen, and an English lad. Off the African coast two of the sailors, Englishmen, died, and a third was left at St. Helena, sick. On Saturday last we were off Falmouth, which port we might have entered but did not ; on Monday, 6 a.m., we were abreast of the Lizard, wind, S.W. to S.S.W. We then came under the land in Mount's Bay, and were tacking about all day, but could not get out." [A vessel had been observed by the Mousehole pilots, on Monday afternoon, endeavouring to get off the eastern land, and about 4 o'clock was seen to 'miss stays' more than once off Mullion Island. She had no signal flying, but it was thought unless she was ably manned she would have great difficulty in rounding the Lizard.] "We hoisted no signal. When the vessel struck every one was on deck, and the Captain cried bitterly. In 20 minutes the vessel broke up. I was on the jib-boom, with two other sailors, and managed to save myself by jumping to the cliff, the others were caught by the sea."

Jury returned verdict—"Accidentally drowned." Just after the inquest, W. Broad, Esq., of Falmouth, Dutch Consul, arrived, bringing with him two Captains of Dutch East Indiamen, then lying at Falmouth. One of them asked at once, " Is it Klaas Lammerts' ?" On being told that the *Kosmopoliet* was the name of the wrecked ship, he said, " He did not believe it, for the *Kosmopoliet* would hardly be due for a fortnight. It must be Klaas Lammerts> vessel, he thought." The Vicar, who had now joined them, exhibited a bit of flannel he had picked up, with " 6, K.L., " marked upon it. " Ah !" said he, "It must be so ! It *must* be the *Jonkheer*." But she had been returned *Kosmo-poliet* at the inquest, on the evidence of the Greek sailor, so there the matter rested.

On the Friday following, however, when Mr Broad and this Dutch Captain again visited Mullyon, the first thing handed them was a parchment which had been picked up, meanwhile, and this was none other than the Masonic diploma of Klaas von Lammerts. Here then was no room for doubt. The ship was identified as the *Jonkheer Meester van de Wall van Puttershoek*, Captain Klaas von Lammerts, 650 tons register, homeward bound from the East Indies, with a cargo of sugar, coffee, spices, and some Banca tin. The value of the ship and cargo would be between £40,000 and £50,000.

The week following the Vicar received a letter from Mrs. C. S., of Manchester, stating that one of the passengers by the ill-fated *Jonkheer* was her sister, Mrs. S. W., 49 years of age, a widow, who had been in India as a governess for 20 years, that her husband had died 9 years ago, and that she was now returning to England, having accumulated a small fortune. From St. Helena, where the vessel had touched on 19th January, her sister had written to her informing her of her being on the passage home. Mrs. S. also made such inquiries as were natural under the circumstances, to which a reply was returned that her sister's remains had been, with others, decently interred in Mullyon churchyard.

Ten more bodies were afterwards recovered and buried.

Tons of coffee were collected and carted away to Penzance, only to prove a ruinous speculation to the purchasers, the salt water had rendered it quite useless. Messrs Jackson and Jones, of Penberth Cove, were engaged to recover the sunken tin, which they did by means of water glasses and long tongs, at a remuneration of £15 per ton. It was found lying with the anchors, chain cables, &c., of the ship, in 6-fathom water. While this work was proceeding, Mr Nicholas, the Consulary agent, at Mullyon, called, one morning, on the Vicar, and asked his company to the Cove, to be present at the opening of a small box, seemingly containing treasure, which Messrs Jackson had fished up. It was a tin box, about a foot square, and contained valuables to the amount of £1200 or £1300.

The Vicar made an inventory of the contents, a list of which is here given.

CONTENTS OF BOX :

Bag—119 two and half guldens,	3 twenty-five guldeh notes,
,, 86 guldens,	1 ,, ,, ,,
10 ten gulden notes,	3 Victoria sovereigns,
13 ,, ,, ,,	5 small pieces silver coin,
1 ,, ,, ,,	2 gold bracelets, 2 brooches,
3 ,, ,, ,,	3 pairs gold earrings, string of beads.

1 two hundred gulden note, Java bank.
1 forty gulden note, Amsterdam bank.
1 seven thousand gulden bill of exchange, in the name Herr A. van D., Rotterdam bank.
1 seven thousand gulden bill of exchange, in the name S. W., Rotterdam bank.
" A Will," by which S. W., leaves all her property to her sister, C. S.
English new Testament, and pocket book.

It contained Mrs. S. W.'s will and property. The discovery of this treasure having been mentioned in the newspapers, another claimant to it, besides Mrs. S., appears on the scene—no less a person than Mrs. W.'s *husband*—supposed to have been dead 9 years ! It appeared that he had separated from her before she went to India, and that he had mysteriously disappeared. Messrs Jackson and Jones received, as was their due, one third of this property ; and, after the law expenses had been paid by Mrs S., and Mrs. W.'s husband, as to the ownership of the remaining two thirds, there was not much left for either to enjoy.

The sum of £5 had been offered by Widow Klaas von Lammerts, of Rue de Plank, Dordrecht, for the recovery of her husband's body, but it was never identified among those washed in.

Cane, bamboo, and wreckage continued to cover every sandy beach for a long time after the wreck.

Coffee bags, laid down as mats, may be now seen on many a cottage lime-ash floor ; sugar baskets, split and fastened to stakes, to protect garden ground, may still be found in many parts of the parish, and this is about all that remains of the ill-fated *Jonkheer*

The almost unaccountable behaviour of this vessel, on the afternoon previous to the wreck, caused grave suspicions in the minds of those on shore that there was mutiny or extreme disorder of some kind on board, but of this nothing certain could be ascertained.

There is, also, a discrepancy in the accounts as to the time of the occurrence of the wreck, which has never been solved satisfactorily. The coast-guard's-man arrived at Mullyon Churchtown about 3 o'clock, a.m., saying he *had seen a large vessel in danger.* That was when the tide had ebbed for four hours. When the villagers went down to the coast they found coffee, and walked over portions of the wreck, which was lying right up at high water

J

mark. The vessel, then, must have struck before or, at least about, the time of high water, and that *was at eleven o'clock the previous evening.*

Was then, after all, the sound, which so startled the Vicar, the last despairing cry of the poor drowning wretches just as the vessel was breaking up?

One saved, 24 drowned—15 buried in Mullyon Churchyard.

The following letters shortly after appeared :—

TO THE EDITOR OF THE WESTERN MORNING NEWS.

SIR,—Upwards of 50 human lives have been lost during the past three months, through lack of a secure anchorage in Mount's Bay for embayed or distressed vessels.

Property in ships and cargoes to the amount of many thousands (£80,000 is probably within the mark) has also been sacrificed from the same cause, and in the same short time. Now, an expenditure of £15,000 would, I am credibly informed, render the Cove at Mullyon a safe harbourage at all states of tide for 20 or 30 vessels.

If this be so, and still no provision be made against such awful shipwrecks as have occurred in Mount's Bay this winter, there will surely be great shortsightedness, to say the least of it, somewhere.

Yours truly,

Mullyon Vicarage, 30th March, 1867.   E. G. HARVEY.

TO THE EDITOR OF THE WEST BRITON.

SIR,—It seems to be a question how many lives must be lost, and what number of vessels wrecked, before any steps are to be taken to provide a place of safety.

It is a very melancholy sight to witness so many human bodies cast on our shore, a prey to the birds and fishes, without an effort being made to prevent such occurrences. Possibly about £20,000 would be all that is required to fill up the gap between Mullyon island and the shore, and extend an arm to the west of the island. which, I venture to say, would be of more use in saving life and property, than the same amount expended anywhere else in England for such a purpose. As for property saved from wrecks, I have been told it is not worth anything to the owners; very often they are brought into debt, and I have every reason to believe it. The valuable cargo of coffee of the Dutch ship *Jonkheer* bids fair to bring its owners into debt. Look at the expensive management--the coastguard, the customs, the police, and their helps are enough to make a wreck of any wreck.

Mullyon, April 13th, 1867.   A.

LAUNCH OF THE MULLYON LIFEBOAT.

Tuesday, the 10th of September, 1867, was the occasion of great festivity at Penzance. There was the opening of the new Public Buildings, the launch of the Mullyon lifeboat, and a lifeboat regatta to follow. Upwards of 10,000 persons were present on the Western Esplanade to witness the launch. The hon. secretary, the committee, and crew had driven over in a four-horse omnibus. After addresses, made by the Rev. E. Nye, the Methodist district chairman ; Mr. Lewis, the secretary to the institution ; and others, the boat was formally handed over ; and bearing the name *Daniel J. Draper*, was at once launched, being welcomed and received by the other five lifeboats, the crews tossing their oars and cheering lustily. On the 13th she was brought over from Penzance to her own station, and then exercised under command of Capt. J. R. Ward, R.N., one of the institution's inspectors.

The Mullyon lifeboat was built in 1867, by Messrs. Forrett, of Limehouse; she is constructed of mahogany, and measures 33 feet in length, by 8 feet 6 inches beam, thus being, with the exception of the Falmouth boat, which is precisely the same size, the largest of the lifeboats on the Cornish coast. She rows 10 oars, and her draught of water is about 23 inches. She is self-righting, and her 6 escape valves admit of her clearing her deck of water almost instantaneously.

The following is the inscription on a marble tablet in the gable of the boat house :—

THIS
LIFEBOAT ESTABLISHMENT
WAS ERECTED IN MEMORY OF THE LATE
REV. DANIEL J. DRAPER,
WHO PERISHED
FROM THE FOUNDERING OF THE
STEAM SHIP " LONDON,"
IN THE BAY OF BISCAY,
ON THE 11TH JANUARY, 1866,
AND WAS PRESENTED TO THE
ROYAL NATIONAL LIFEBOAT INSTITUTION,
BY WESLEYAN METHODISTS,
THROUGH THE MEDIUM OF THE
" METHODIST RECORDER " NEWSPAPER,
CONDUCTED BY THE REV. LUKE WISEMAN
AND MR. THOMAS SMITH,
1867.
C. H. COOKE, ESQ., F.R.I.B.A., HON. ARCHITECT.

IMPROVEMENT OF THE COVE.

About this time, extensive operations were carried on at Porthmellin, by way of widening the entrance and improving the beach as a launching and landing place ; through the instrumentality of the Lifeboat Institution, a large quantity of obstructive rocks were blown up and removed from the former, while from the latter, the fresh-water stream which had hitherto denuded the shingle of sand, was diverted by means of an artificial water-course of stone erected for the purpose on the north side of the Cove. The result has been a success, not only as regards the lifeboat and her movements, but also as giving increased accommodation for fishing boats, and what is of even greater consequence, as securing greater safety to all whilst launching or beaching during rough weather.

WRECK OF THE "ACHILLES."

The lifeboat had occupied her allotted station for a little more than a month, when evidence only too palpable was afforded of the wisdom which dictated the selection of the coast of Mullyon as the scene of her labours. The London newspapers of 23rd October, 1867, contained the following paragraph :—

Mullyon, Tuesday, 22nd October, 3.30 a.m. "I have much gratification (says the Rev. E. G. Harvey) in reporting the first and successful service of the *Daniel J. Draper*. At 10 o'clock last night, during foul weather and a thick fog, the alarm was given that a vessel was in distress off Polurrian Cove. The lifeboat was thereupon promptly launched, and was, fortunately, the means of saving three of the men from the stranded vessel. The coastguard men, who had been the first to observe her, had, meanwhile, been able to save the remaining 15 men, by means of the rocket apparatus. The ship was the *Achilles*, of Glasgow, Capt. David Kinnear, bound from Miramichi to London, with a cargo of timber. Other vessels are reported to be in danger, so it is possible that the services of the lifeboat may again be called into requisition."

Our coxswain offered to take out a warp to seaward, so as to prevent the ship being lifted further in on to the beach, but this was declined by the captain. The following day, he was advised to throw overboard his deck cargo, but he contented himself with removing such valuables as he was able, together with sails, &c., and sent for tug steamers. He was told they would be useless unless he cleared his deck—but probably he was a Scotchman. The tugs came and tugged in vain, the vessel was immoveable, and there she lay partially embedded in the sand for weeks, as the wind continued for a long period to blow off shore, and the sea was comparatively calm. She gradually went to pieces, however, while the greater part of her cargo was secured and sold by auction on the spot.

WRECK OF THE "MARIA LOUISA."

The next catastrophe on my list is one which presents as great a contrast as may be. Tuesday, 21st January, 1868. Once more a terribly wild and stormy night, followed by a morning as severe. A complete hurricane was blowing, only to be equalled by the terrific gale of 1865. The wind roaring as if it had never blown before, carried up with it flakes of sea foam far in land, and the sea itself was lashed into a scene of frightful grandeur—the waves plunging against and leaping up the bold precipices of the cliffs, and the spray being carried well aloft whenever a submerged rock or point of land obstructed the progress of the furious element. To hold one's own—to stand against the the force of the wind without support, was a sheer impossibility ; and on the cliff, if you had hold of a rock for shelter, it was all you could do to prevent your being blown away from that. In the midst of this howling storm, a smack of about 80 or 90 tons was discovered about a couple of miles N.W. of Mullyon Island. To have attempted to launch the lifeboat in such tremendous billows as were now thundering in at the Cove, and in the teeth of such a gale, would have been but folly ; but the rocket apparatus was, after great difficulty, brought down to the shore. The devoted little craft came driving along under close reefed mainsail and storm jib, half buried in the masses of wave upon wave through which she was being impelled. A terrible sight to see a frail thing like this rushing on to inevitable destruction. No human form could be descried on board of her, yet on she came until she seemed to be driven half under water by some invisible power to her final goal. Three tremendous seas followed one upon the other with terrible fury, and there she struck, even while sinking, upon Treguin, a rock on the northern part of the island. In less than two minutes no remains of her were to be seen. Yet shortly afterwards, on the beach at Polurrian, were found a bit of stern piece with

" A., PADSTOW " painted upon it ; a basket containing a Guernsey frock, and sundry bits of linen ; a blanket and a blue worsted stocking.

These were the relics left to the owners—the widows and orphans of the little company of the *Maria Louisa* of Padstow. All hands—3 drowned, 2 buried in Mullyon churchyard.

THE " CALCUTTA'S " LIFEBOAT.

On February 9th, 1869, at 9 o'clock a.m., during a gale from S.W., a ship's lifeboat, about 28 feet long, was discovered on the beach at Pedn y Ké, between Polurrian and Porthmellin, with her bows stove in, but otherwise uninjured ; there were several bags of clothing found with her, and a lifebuoy attached bearing the name *Calcutta*, London. The tidings which reached us during the few days following only partially solved the mysterious appearance of this boat. It appeared that on Sunday, the 7th, the *Calcutta*, a full-rigged iron ship of 2,000 tons, having on board some 250 miles of telegraph cable for the Persian Gulf, with 52 hands as crew, and 12 perons in charge of the cable ; when about 150 miles S.W. of the Lizard, came in collision with the barque *Emma*, of Memel, bound from Cardiff for Barcelona, with 500 tons of coal on board. The *Emma* sank within three minutes of the collision, and her mate, the cook and two boys were hauled on board the *Calcutta*, the Captain and six men were drowned, going down with the vessel. The *Calcutta* herself was also seriously damaged, and it was soon found that water was gaining upon them, spite of the steam pumps that were kept constantly at work. The Captain having headed her towards the western coast, held on his course as well as he could, her steering gear having become disabled, but ordered the boats to be got in readiness. The next day, the crew considering the vessel was in a sinking condition, demanded of the Captain what he intended doing. He replied that he would hold on for a couple of hours longer, and then he would see what could be done. At 2 o'clock he called all aft, and three vessels being seen to leeward, some determined to put off to them in the boats. Fifteen men then got into one of the boats under command of the third mate, and another boat took 8 men more. This second boat came in on the shore between Penzance and Marazion the same night, about 10 o'clock, and the men landed, having no notion where they were. Those in the first boat were picked up about 4 in the afternoon, just off the Wolf Rock, by a Greek vessel, the *Crissophigi*, and with the exception of two, who were drowned in the attempt to get on board the Greek ship, were landed that night at Falmouth. About two hours after, the lifeboat, with 21 hands on board, left the ship. Whilst she was being lowered, the mate was knocked into the ship's hold, where he lay as if dead. The last boat, which was the Captain's gig, was then lowered with 13 hands, he insisting on doing this himself. The rope slipped out of his hands, and the boat throwing out her living cargo into the sea, was herself smashed against the side of the vessel, and thus 10 more were drowned, the Captain himself among the number.

Eight hands only were now left on board, an insufficient number undoubtedly to work the ship. They were taken off on the morning of the 9th, and landed at Falmouth. As a specimen of the work that is commonly performed by our Cornish lifeboats, I quote the following from the columns of the *Western Morning News :*—

The Rev. F. C. Jackson, Hon. Secretary of the Cadgwith lifeboat branch, thus describes the success of the Cadgwith lifeboat :—He says " There was a terrible sea running on our beach, and the coxswain and crew were told that it was risking life to launch the boat in such a surf, yet they embarked and went out in the teeth of the storm. Before them lay, some seven or nine miles distant, this helpless and then unknown hulk, with inverted ensign flying. On nearing the wreck, so glad were the crew of the *Calcutta* to see our boat, and in it the prospect of escape, that they hailed with cheers her arrival. They needed no persuasion to induce them to quit the vessel, imprisoned as they had been without means of escape, should the ship founder as was momentarily anticipated by the crew. It was no easy matter to go alongside the *Calcutta ;* bits of wire rigging were hanging all round her, which it was impossible to cut, had the boat been driven by the sea among it. I know not how the boat of the *Terrible* managed, but we must bear in mind that they did their work twenty-two hours after the lifeboat, during which time the weather had improved, and the ship had drifted twenty miles to the eastward. Besides, they had not that great moral difficulty to contend with, viz. :—the fact of no help being near should any accident happen. There was no desire on the part of the crew to save anything but life, and though some of those who quitted the *Calcutta* wished to bring off their luggage, our coxswain, not knowing how many men might crowd in, steadfastly refused, not wishing to hamper our boat in so heavy a sea, and so strong a gale. Neither would he allow any one to board the ship, though it was said by the saved that there was plenty of everything on board, if the crew would like to take it. The crew of the *Western Commercial Traveller* lifeboat has added another feather to that glorious cap of valour which belongs, of right and might, to those gallant men who, all round the coasts of England, do deeds of bravery and self-devotion under the kind and benevolent direction of the Royal National Lifeboat Institution."

The Rev. P. Vyvyan Robinson, Hon. Secretary of the Lizard Lifeboat, writes :—"Early on Tuesday morning, I was informed that a large ship was in distress six miles off the Lizard Lighthouse. There was some delay in getting things ready to launch, for the Lifeboat had to be brought from Polpeer to Church Cove, and the crew had to be collected from some distance. When all was ready, I was told that the Cadgwith boat had been gone some time, but I decided to send out the boat, as from the great size of the vessel, it was probable that she might contain more persons than could be brought off by one boat, in one trip. The launch was easily affected about 9.30 a.m., and and we watched the course of the boat under sail through the heavy water with the naked eye, and with glasses, until through the deep haze, she and the vessel were lost to sight. I give you the details, therefore, from the coxswain's narrative. He said, " We steered S.E. by S. and soon met with a tremendous sea, two waves in succession broke over the boat, swamping us all, and only the drogue saved us. About five miles from land, our sailing being slow, from the drogue being out, we sighted the ship right ahead, and reached her about two hours and a half after leaving the shore. We went round her twice and shouted loudly, but there was no reply ; so thinking her abandoned, and apparently in a sinking state, we resolved to make for Falmouth Harbour. The sea was still very heavy, continually sweeping the boat, but she behaved most gallantly, and the drogue kept her straight. In about two hours of very smart sailing, we sighted land, which eventually proved to be Pendennis Castle. Soon after, we reached Gerrans Bay, and then tacked and reached the entrance of the Harbour. Here our sails became useless, and while we were vainly struggling to row in against the wind and tide, a tug came out and took us in. We landed at 8 p.m., and were most kindly cared for by Mr. Webber, the chairman of the Falmouth lifeboat.' One cannot but admire the energy, perseverance, skill, and endurance shewn by the crew, and the wonderful aptitude of the boat for such perilous work. The men were out more than ten hours, frequently drenched by the sweeping waves, with no refreshment of any kind, and yet their confidence in the boat and themselves never wavered. Surely such men and such vessels will, under God, do anything that should be expected from mortal strength and skill."

Three steam tugs now put out from Falmouth in search of the *Calcutta*, and one of these, the *Dandy*, fell in with her and made an attempt to take her in tow, but her tow rope being of insufficient strength to bear the strain of its unwieldy burden, and in such a heavy sea, she was obliged to abandon her. H.M.S. *Terrible*, paddle-wheel steamer, had also been sent out in search of the *Calcutta*, but had overshot her while she continued to drift up channel. On the report of the *Dandy* as to her whereabouts, the *Terrible* again put out on the hunt after the derelict, and at length, on the morning of the 10th, came upon her about 10 miles off the Eddystone. But derelict she was no longer. They found Glyn, the Plymouth pilot on board, though alone. The bold fellow had resolved to take charge of her as well as he could by himself, while his cutter returned to Plymouth with the tidings. The *Terrible* then, after much difficulty in clearing the wreck of her encumbering gear, took her in tow, and after encountering some danger at the entrance of the Sound, by reason of the loss of the *Calcutta's* rudder, at length anchored her inside the Breakwater.

The value of the vessel with her cargo was estimated at £250,000, and after she had been well overhauled, strong opinions were expressed on the course taken by the ship's company in leaving her ; although she was much damaged, there was no sufficient reason for abandoning the ship.

But all this time, what has become of the 21 who left her in her lifeboat? As no tidings of them came to hand, it was supposed that they had been taken on board some outward-bound vessel, and that they had deserted the lifeboat, particularly as her rowlocks shewed little signs of having been long used—we

K

should be sure to hear something of them in a few days. But days passing by and no tidings arriving, the opinion gained ground that few were the tidings that would ever be told.

A month after (March 5th,) the body of a man, much mutilated, was found floating off Predannack head. Another month passed, and on the 8th of April, there was washed ashore at Polurrian, the body of a young man, his clothes and all about him sound, while the poor head, bereft of flesh and hair, was completely bleached.

The state of suspense in which the relatives of these poor fellows were all this time placed, was pitiable in the extreme ; and the Vicar was in almost daily receipt of letters revealing their heart-rending anxiety, their fearful doubt, their tenacious hope against hope. " Unless we obtain certain evidence of their loss, we cannot but cherish a hope of their safety." " I hope you will perse- vere in your endeavours to solve this sad mystery." " Did you ever know so large a number lost, or so many to be so long sanded." " Do you not think it remarkable that, while two of the crew of the gig had come ashore, no positive evidence of even one of the lifeboat has been found, though they were 21 to 10 in the gig." " We are still sanguine, tho' as time creeps on and we get no tidings, our hopes seem to decrease." " Anything that would lead to identification would set our minds at rest." were words that reached him.

On the 14th of April, more than two months after the lifeboat had left her ship, some human remains, in an undescribable state, came into Porth Mellin. The Vicar took some specimens of the rotting clothing, and found one portion marked " E.D." (He had been supplied previously with the list of the names of those who left the *Calcutta* in her lifeboat.) He communicated with the father of Evan Davis, who identified these relics as having belonged to his son. But the matter was not yet settled. The surviving mate declared that Evan Davis was lost out of the Captain's gig, and was not one of the company of the lifeboat. After much further correspondence, however, the Vicar received the following letter from Davis' father :—" I have had information from two young men from this neighbourhood, who were among the last in the *Calcutta*. My son was seen by both leaving in the lifeboat with another from this neigh- bourhood. This settles for ever the fate of the 21."

And nothing further has come to light concerning them. It is supposed that the boat must have capsized just outside, or that she struck on Mullyon Island, when all were probably drowned at once, then buried in the sand below for many weeks, when the sea began gradually to give up their remains.

21 drowned, 4 buried in Mullyon Churchyard.

THE PARSON'S WORK AT A WRECK.

When I have spoken to an inland friend of the labours that accrue to the Parson at and after a wreck, it has been often asked me, with some expression of surprise, " What can there be for you, particularly, to do on such an occasion?" The fact is that the Parson's work, at such a time is always anxious, often arduous, especially if he be the Hon. Secretary to a Lifeboat Branch, as is the case with the three most southerly situated clergymen in England. I need not here speak of his lifeboat work, nor need I but allude to the manner in which he will, by personal example and influence, exert himself at the actual time of a wreck ; but, and it is as well to draw attention to the fact, the relatives and friends of the shipwrecked mariner on these shores, know well that within some short distance of the spot there will be the resident parochial clergyman, a man of education, and one, presumably from his office, possessed of more than ordinary feelings of humanity and Christian charity. To him, therefore, they address their early enquiries concerning their loved ones ; to him they express their griefs or their hopes ; and, feeling they can do so with greater freedom than they could to the owners of the vessel, the customs' officers, or the receivers of wreck, to him they look for sympathy and advice ; and he, on his part, can but feel it his duty, in every way, to sympathise with the survivors, to condole with the bereaved, and to use his best efforts in endeavouring to identify the remains, however mutilated, of every poor battered body that is washed on shore, or found afloat. This last, being no one's *official* work, he finds himself, as it were, morally compelled to do all he can ; to carefully inspect the body of every drowned person, and to take notes of clothing, hair, marks, or anything by means of which the deceased may be recognised. Thus it happens, as in the case of the 21 of the *Calcutta's* boat, that his voluntary labours are the means of ascertaining the fate of many whose actual end would otherwise have remained doubtful.

Again, the parson, in the course of this correspondence, becomes often the depository of heartrending narratives, the details of which, probably, remain unknown to the officials, as, for instance, in the case of the *Boyne*, when he is begged by a widowed mother, who has, but recently, lost her husband at sea, to be particular in his watch for the remains of her son, her only son, who was her only earthly means of support; or when he is requested to give all possible information to, and accompany in their daily search on the spot, the relatives of an unfortunate apprentice lad, who, although he had escaped drowning after falling overboard in a gale off the Cape of Good Hope, comes close home to meet his death.

The parson has his reward, doubtless, as he pictures to himself, weeks, perhaps, after all traces of the ship and her cargo have disappeared, the reception, by the grieving relatives, of some such communication, from himself, as the following—which is a true copy—" I had, my dear Madam, the melancholy satisfaction of committing to our hallowed ground, and with our accustomed rites, the remains of your poor drowned brother, having been enabled to identify the body by the symbols you described as marked on his left arm—viz., a cross, anchor and heart, with the initials ' A.S.L.' "

Or again, when the bodies are washed in soon after the striking of the ship, and they await the coroner's inquest, or their removal to a distance for burial, the parson, on a remote coast like this, from his necessarily frequent visits to the remains, seems, to himself at least, to have almost known them personally when alive, and their peaceful countenances are imprinted on his mental vision, for a long time afterwards, with a distinctness beyond that of many a well-known friend.

But the frequent occurrence of these scenes do not increase his love for the sea.   He comes, at times, to look upon that vast element, particularly when lashed into fury in a storm, as a huge and greedy monster, that will, if it have the opportunity, lick and lap you to destruction within its insatiable maw, or beat the life-breath out of you by hurling you against its iron barriers.

WRECK OF THE " REMEDY."

On the 22nd of April, 1869, the schooner *Remedy*, 140 tons register, belonging to Mr. C. Holt, of Whitstable, Kent, Captain J. Bonchar, with a cargo of coals, from Cardiff for Caen, went ashore near Predannack Point. The master and crew saved themselves without assistance, and the vessel soon went to pieces.

WRECK OF THE "BERTHE AND LEONTINE."

On the 27th of January, 1871, the Captain of *Berthe and Leontine*, French brig, being in a fog to the southward of Mullyon Island, fancied he was in danger of foundering, and, with his crew of five men, left his vessel in their boat, by which they reached Kynance Cove, and safely landed. The vessel was found lifted by the waves on to a ledge or terrace of rock, near Mên te heul, where the receding tide left her in a perfectly upright position, with her masts, sails, and rigging all in perfect order. She was soon cleared of all valuables, and then left to the mercy of the sea. The result need hardly be mentioned.

FATAL ACCIDENT TO A MULLYON FISHING-BOAT.

A sad accident, by which four lives were lost, occurred to a Mullyon fishing-boat, on Friday, April 19th, 1872, which, while it cast a deep gloom over the whole of the little community among whom the unfortunate deceased resided, and while it rendered desolate the home of one poor woman, already a widow, also deprived another mother of five children of their chief comforter and means of support. William Mundy, a man whose life had been spent in the fishery along this dangerous coast, and therefore an experienced boatman, together with two of his sons and another young man, left Mullyon Cove on the Friday morning, in his open fishing-boat, for Porthleven, in order to fetch some nets which were awaiting him there. The morning was fine, with a moderate breeze from N.N.E., and the water, therefore, comparatively smooth over the greater part of their course. They had proceeded to within a mile of the pier at Porthleven, when, standing in on her last tack, the boat was observed by some persons on the shore, suddenly to lose way, and in a few moments to disappear altogether. That those on board were aware of their danger was evident, for they were engaged in lowering the sail when the boat sank. Immediately, on the first symptom of disablement, three boats were urged out with all speed to the spot, under oars and canvas, reaching the scene of the catastrophe in less than ten minutes; but, alas! nothing whatever was to be seen either of the boat or of the men. From the shore, by the aid of a telescope, one poor fellow was seen to struggle on the surface for about two minutes, but all were lost. A hat, a coat, a bag, a pair of oars, and a boat's bucket were found floating about, the last of these being the only thing by which the unhappy craft could be identified. The hat was sent on to Mullyon at once by a passing boat, which also brought the sad intelligence that the men were drowned. The hat was recognised as belonging to one of the party, but as a hat might easily have been blown off without further accident, and as the day was so fine, and Mundy such a well-known experienced hand, many at Mullyon refused to credit the story of his boat's having sunk. The return of messengers, however, later in the afternoon, confirmed the sad truth of the first report—All were drowned.

Various were the conjectures as to the cause of the boat's sinking, but of these, the most probable would seem to be that the "step" of the mast giving way, a plank was thus forced out of the boat's bottom, and thus, without capsizing, she gradually filled and sank, and taking with her her unfortunate occupants. The names of the poor fellows were William Mundy, aged 58; his sons, Joel, 25, and Henry, 13; and a friend, John Henry Williams, aged 20. The last-named young man, who was a carpenter at Mullyon, living with a widowed step-mother, was shortly to have been married—a pitiable case enough! but poor Mundy's fate is even more distressing. The brave coxswain of the *Daniel J. Draper* Mullyon Lifeboat, deservedly respected by all with whom he came in contact, who, in his occupation as fisherman along this rugged coast, had lived a life of peril, had often braved the storm and saved the lives of others, thus under a bright sky and in a smooth sea, together with two of his sons, at length yields up his life to the element he so long had battled.

The bodies of the three men were found in about two to six weeks after the accident, and their remains interred in Mullyon Churchyard; the poor little boy never appeared again.

The Vicar set on foot a subscription on behalf of Mundy's widow and his remaining children, and, chiefly by the aid of the Royal National Lifeboat

Institution, the subscribers to the Mullyon Lifeboat, and other Wesleyan friends, he was enabled to collect about £100 for them. One of the younger children was also placed in the Orphan Home, at Brixham.

THE WOLF ROCK LIGHTHOUSE.

We had held great hopes of the efficacy of the splendid new light in the Wolf Rock in warning homeward bound vessels from this great natural ' trap' of Mount's Bay, which lies ever open to engulph the unwary. This lighthouse, which is erected on a rock of peculiar formation, was opened for the first time on the 1st January, 1871. There was once an attempt made to fix on the top of this rock the huge figure of a wolf in copper, whose open mouth, receiving the winter's blast, should terrify or warn the sailor of his peril. This Chinese phantasy soon succumbed to the first south-wester, and is now replaced by one of the finest lights on the coast. The rock itself, situated 8 miles from the Land's End and 22 from the Lizard, is a pillar of almost basaltic origin, shooting up from beneath in the form of a pinnacle, since within a radius of a cable's length you at once get 30 fathoms of water all round. There was a very good model of the lighthouse exhibited at the International Museum, South Kensington, in 1873. Its height above water is about 100 feet, the light shewing an alternate red and white flash with the interval of a minute. We see it, though 23 miles distant, from our Vicarage windows, any night when the weather is not positively hazy, and doubtless it has been the means of warning many from the dangers of this rugged coast ; but not all, unfortunately.

THE WRECK OF THE " BOYNE."

At Trenance farm, Mullyon, at 5.45, on the morning of the 1st of March, 1873, Thomas Jacka, the farmer, was just arousing himself from his slumber, when, happening to cast a cursory glance toward his window, he beheld a rocket-signal of distress shooting across the wintry sky. Hastily throwing about him a few articles of clothing, he hurried out towards the edge of the cliff, which at this point rises some 200 feet above the level of the sea, and through the dim light of the early morning, now rendered more obscure than usual by a thick fog and driving rain, he fancied he could perceive in the distance to the northward a vessel on the rocks. He hurried back to inform his cousin, who rapidly dressed, and both of them with all speed proceeded along the coast in the direction of the ship, passing on their way, as they needs must, the deep valley, at the mouth of which lies Polurrian Cove. Ascending the opposite hill, and going on for about a quarter of a mile along the edge of the cliff, they saw at a spot called the "Merres Ledges" (itself the scene of many a former wreck) a large barque on the rocks, about fifteen fathoms from the cliff, lying broadside on to the sea and partly covered with the waves. Then hearing the cries of those on board, for they could not as yet, owing to the thickness of the weather, discover any human form, Jacka immediately hastened to the Church Town to give the alarm, calling first on Mr. White, the chief boatman of the coastguard, and next on Samuel Mundy, the second coxswain of the life-boat. It was now more than a quarter past six o'clock, and the unfortunate vessel had been bumping and grinding on the rocks where she first had struck for more than an hour. White got out the rocket apparatus and called together his staff of assistants, and Mundy, sending messengers to collect his crew, hastened to the Vicarage to speak the Hon. Secretary, and then ran off to Mullyon Cove to launch the lifeboat.

Hurrying with all speed to the scene of the wreck, White planted his apparatus on the most available spot on the top of the cliff, at about 150 yards from the vessel. She was now lying partially dismasted on her port side, which was partly under water, the other portion of the ship being every now and then submerged in the advancing breakers. At this moment there were seven men observed on different parts of the vessel, three of whom were suddenly swept off by a huge wave. One of these poor fellows, who afterwards turned out to be the Captain, was seen for some time swimming about by the aid of a life-buoy, but the other two quickly disappeared. The rocket was fired and its rope fell among the four remaining men, the vessel now showing signs of rapidly breaking up. The rope was caught by one of the men, and he alone slowly hauled out the double line. The block of this got jammed, and the line itself twisted when the cry of "The Lifeboat" echoed along the cliff. The poor fellow then gave up his attempt to make use of the rocket line, which was now so twisted that those on shore could no longer work it. Dropping into the sea, it was eagerly seized by the man in the life-buoy, who having seen the rocket fired, had attempted to get near the vessel. In his attempt he was carried in by the waves between the vessel and the rocks, and now he endeavoured to haul himself in by the rope, hand over hand, to the cliff. He was beckoned off, making his way as he was to certain destruction, but he took no heed of the kindly warning. Had he kept further away he would undoubtedly have been picked up by the lifeboat, but slipping his hold on the rope, he fell once more into the surging waters, and although a line was thrown to him from the top of the cliff, and he seemed to catch it for a moment, he quickly sank to rise no more.

While this was going on, the lifeboat had anchored about 60 yards to windward of the vessel, which had now broken in two, fore and aft; and while the lifeboat was dropping down to near the wreck, two out of the four that remained of the unfortunate crew were washed off, one of them hanging for some considerable time over the leeward side of the vessel; but from his position he could not be seen by those on board the lifeboat, and therefore no attempt was made by her to come between the vessel and the cliff to save him. The poor fellows themselves were so utterly benumbed and exhausted by their long exposure to the terrible waves, that they seemed incapable of doing anything to save themselves.

On the first opportunity Sam Mundy threw the leaded-cane line to one of the two remaining unfortunates, but it fouled; another line was immediately thrown and caught, the man who caught it twisting it around his arm and his body, and then, to the astonishment and horror of the lifeboat's crew, also round one of his legs and the rail of the ship. Another line was at once thrown to the other man. He caught it, and was engaged in fastening it round himself when a breaker washed him off his hold on to the sloping deck of the vessel, and under her wheel, where getting jammed by the force of the breakers, he lost his hold of the line, was carried off by the succeeding wave, and drowned. The stern portion of the vessel, on which the only survivor now stood, parted from the rest of the ship, it rolled over, and he too disappeared in the greedy waves.

The attention of those on shore was now directed to a small boat, which had not before been seen, coming in from seaward, the occupants of which pulled straight in to Mullyon Cove. These were three of the crew of the wrecked vessel, Griffiths, Parsons, and Wilkinson, with an apprentice lad, Davidson,* on board. They had seen the lifeboat putting out, and naturally concluded that the spot whence she was launched was one where they could land. The interest of the lifeboat's crew, and indeed of all the spectators, had been hitherto so absorbed in the illfated vessel herself, that this boat had not been noticed until she was close in shore. The little party were in a most exhausted state, after battling with the waves, and alternately pulling and bailing out their small craft; but after getting into dry clothing, which was sent them from the Vicarage, and being otherwise cared for, they were able to give the following particulars of the sad disaster. They said their vessel was an iron-built barque, named *The Boyne*, of Scarborough, belonging to Messrs. Tyndall and Co., 617 tons register, John Whelan, master, with a crew of 19 all told. She was just 120 days home from Samarang, bound to Falmouth for orders, having a valuable cargo of 900 tons of sugar. All had gone well with them up to the time of her striking. On 28th February, at 4 p.m., they had sighted the Scillies, and a little later the Wolf Rock Light, which was then on her port bow. At 7.30 the Lizard Lights were seen. At 8 o'clock all hands were called to shorten sail, and the ship was kept close to the wind. At 11.30 the ship was put on the port tack, the Lizard then bearing E.N.E. 15 miles on the starboard quarter. At one a.m., and again at 2.30, soundings were taken; at 3 o'clock she was put on the starboard tack, wind W.S.W., blowing half a gale, weather thick and hazy, no light visible. At 4.15 the master went below, leaving the deck in charge of the second officer. At about 5 a.m. a crash arising from the bowsprit was the first warning of anything being wrong, and a moment afterwards, the vessel running at about 9 or 10 knots at the time, suddenly struck on the rocks, and was immediately thrown round broadside on to the waves in a perfectly helpless state. So utterly unaware was every one on board of approaching danger that some were comfortably preparing breakfast, all expecting to be in Falmouth Harbour soon after daybreak.

*It may be mentioned here as a curious coincidence that the apprentice lad, Davidson, one of the saved, was on his next voyage again wrecked off the Coast of Cornwall, Island of Jamaica, and again rescued, being thus twice wrecked and twice saved within a twelve month, off "the Coast of Cornwall;" and that the Captain of *The Boyne* was the last of three brothers who had met their deaths by drowning.

The Captain seemed to realize his position at once. They had sailed right against Mullyon Cliffs, when they had imagined they were well clear of the Lizard, and making in for Falmouth. He ordered the boats at once to be lowered, and these three men and the boy had managed to get into the boat that had brought them ashore after she had been let down from the windward side of the vessel. They stayed alongside for some time endeavouring to persuade the Captain to join them, but he refused, and told them they had better pull away for the land, his last words being ' Good luck to you.' What happened to the other boats no one knew, and they were never seen by anyone afterwards. These four then pulled about, hoping to find Falmouth, when at last they saw the lifeboat in the distance, and then they made for the shore where they had seen her come out. They had saved their own lives, but otherwise had lost their all, and in a few hours they had sufficiently recovered to visit the scene of the wreck. They had had courage and fortitude sufficient to trust their lives in the small boat in which they left the vessel, but the scene before them now broke them down, and they fairly wept at the sight of it. All signs of their comrades had disappeared, and with them the whole of the cargo, save the empty sugar baskets which were floating about in hundreds. The fore part of the ship still held together, but the deck and linings had been twisted and thrown about in all directions, rigging, tackles, spars, and other gear having been broken up and washed away by the receding tide. And thus the master, both mates, and 12 of the crew were lost, adding 15 more souls to the sad list of ' the drowned at Mullyon.'

The body of the Captain was soon after washed in, and being recognised by friends was removed for burial, just after the coroner's inquest, to Hull ; and the bodies of seven of the crew (amongst which were identified those of two apprentices, John Clark and Alexander Lowe Grahame) were washed ashore at various intervals, and buried in Mullyon Churchyard.

A Board of Trade Inquiry as to the cause of the disaster was afterwards instituted at the earnest request of a relation of Grahame's, the result being the delivery of the following opinion :—

" It appeared to the Court that the fatal mistake the master made, was tacking to the northward at 11.30 on the night of 28th February."

15 drowned—7 buried in Mullyon Churchyard.

The following letter appeared in a Plymouth newspaper, on 14th March, 1873 :—

TO THE EDITOR OF THE WESTERN MORNING NEWS.

Sir,—The ineffective look-out kept on board vessels, especially in the channel or near the coast, is becoming more and more notorious, and those on shore have often to bear the blame which is really due to those on board. The Barque *Boyne*, wrecked here on the 1st instant is, I fear, another instance of this kind. It was a dirty night, but nothing like a gale blowing, and the barque *Boyne* having already sighted the Wolf Light and the Lizard on the previous evening, instead of getting into Falmouth, whither she was bound, at 5.20 a.m. strikes against our cliffs and shortly becomes a total wreck, with a loss of 15 lives.

True, she was not observed from the shore by any one till more than an hour after she struck. No fault of the Coastguard watchman surely, when it is considered that he has to guard no less than seven miles of such a coast as this, taking at least four hours at this time of the year to walk or rather scramble over his beat. On this occasion the watchman had not long before passed the very spot where this wreck occurred. And at the inquest held here yesterday the evidence of independent witnesses established the fact very clearly that the coastguard had done their duty both on watch and with the rocket apparatus, and that the crew of the Lifeboat had done all that men could do to rescue the drowning. But ! one watchman, or even as there are often, two to guard such a coast as this in thick weather? Would this be a sufficient coastguard anywhere out of Cornwall? Five years ago I gave my opinion of this matter to a Commanding Inspector of Coastguards, and received as a reply, that I was not in a position to form an opinion. Perhaps not, I have a strong one, nevertheless. And if these lines should happen to meet the eye of any captain or master of a vessel, let me entreat him, for his own sake and for the sake of his crew, to keep a good look-out,—for, in a storm a quarter of an hour will often suffice, if he should find himself on our cliffs, to smash his vessel to bits, and to drown every soul on board.

In six years and a quarter there have been nine wrecks, with a loss of sixty-nine lives, under Mullyon cliffs, on a bit of coast line not more than a mile and a half in length, and more than a hundred lives lost out of thirteen wrecks in ten years.

Yours truly,
E. G. HARVEY,

March 8, 1873.   Vicar of Mullyon and Hon. Sec. Mullyon Lifeboat Branch.

TELEGRAPH.

In May, 1873, a memorial influentially signed, was forwarded to the Post Office authorities in the hope of securing telegraphic communication to Mullyon, but without success. It is to be hoped, however, that such extension will not be much longer delayed. The telegraph of this "bright little tight little island" of ours can never be considered at all complete until there is direct communication from one coastguard station to another, or from lifeboat branch to lifeboat branch along the whole coast.

Our memorial and the result will be found in the Appendix.

WRECK OF THE "DIANA."

The Austrian barque *Diana*,* of Piccolo Lossini, 535 tons register, Captain

---

* Although this wreck did not occur on the coasts of this parish, I have been so repeatedly urged to insert it among the others that I could not well refuse to admit this account of it.

Bonifacio Cattarinich, laden with wheat, left Falmouth for Dublin early on
Tuesday morning, 8th December, 1874, weather thick and stormy.   Encountering the full force of a southwesterly gale about eight miles S.W. off the
Wolf Rock Lighthouse, she had some of her canvas blown away, which rendered it necessary for her to return to Falmouth to refit.   The attempt to clear
the Lizard, however, failed, and at 3.30 she was on the sands and in the surf
in Gunwalloe Church Cove.   At about three o'clock she was seen in the haze
off Mullyon Cliffs, a very heavy and awkward sea running into Mount's Bay
at the time.   The rocket apparatus was got out, and the Lifeboat's crew were
soon ready, when the vessel, which had been lost sight of for a few minutes,
owing to the thickness of the mist, was again seen off Mullyon Island, where
from some cause she was compelled to wear ship; this made her fate more
speedy of accomplishment, and it was now only a question on what particular
spot she would come on shore, that it might not be against the cliffs was the hope
of all.   It was a sad, yet awfully splendid sight to witness the fine ship proudly
rushing along in her wild career through and over the whitened waves, under
and almost close to the lofty cliffs, nearer and nearer at every moment, to
swift and inevitable destruction.   And the poor souls on board !   How many ?
Will they escape ? Be drowned ?   Or killed against the rocks ?   Heaven help
them ! A signal gun is fired.   Ah ! no need for that now ! It seems like
mockery to us who know from an only too long and sad experience the nature
of the impending catastrophe.   About four minutes and she nears Poljew, but,
clearing this, she strikes on the sand at Church Cove, where she lies stern on
to the breakers, which soon deluge her in foam.

The rocket apparatus is planted and a line fired, but it misses her.   A
second is fired.   " Well done Philip Angel !"   It falls right between her main
and mizen masts, but becoming entangled in the rigging does not reach the
deck, and before they can secure it a third line is fired which falls across the
poop.   This is easily caught, and by it the hawser hauled out, and immediately
is the cradle sent out on its errand of mercy.   It brings in first the Captain's
wife, and then the Captain, who was so exhausted as to require support on his
way to the nearest farm house ; after that the crew in couples to the number
of 12 were taken off, until the mate alone was left, and then he too is hauled

to shore in safety amid the grateful cheers of the assembled spectators. The crew, who had left their all on board, were clothed temporarily by the fishermen and villagers of the neighbourhood; and then taken for the night, some to Gunwalloe fishing village and some to Mullyon Churchtown, where they were made as comfortable as circumstances would allow.

The Coastguard men and their assistants, under command of Mr. Harris, officer of Coastguard, Mullyon, deserve all praise for their prompt and energetic behaviour with the rocket apparatus. The rapidity with which it was brought to bear on the unfortunate ship's company, and the complete success which attended their efforts, were matters of sincere congratulation to all. The *Diana* lay perfectly upright across the Cove for some weeks afterwards, and while her cargo was being taken out, which was done without difficulty as she was often left dry by the receding tide, hopes were entertained of her being once more floated off, and she was purchased as she lay for £300; but heavy weather coming on about the middle of January her starboard bilge gave in first of all, and in about a week her remains were to be seen arranged in piles along the beach awaiting the arrival of the auctioneer.

THE OLD CORNISH LANGUAGE.

F all the varied dialects of the ancient Celtic or Gaelic tongue, such as is the Welsh, Irish, Manx, Armoric, or Cornish, the latter seems to have been the purest. In early times the Cornish more nearly approximated the Welsh in construction ; but later, by reason doubtless of the more frequent intercourse which existed between the inhabitants of the coasts of Cornwall and Brittany, the Cornish and the Armoric were more nearly allied in grammar and pronounciation. This will be seen by comparing the Apostles' Creed as given below in Cornish of different dates, with the Welsh and Armoric versions.

Of these three dialects the Cornish has always been held the most elegant and expressive, as Carew says, " It is not so unpleasing in sound with throat letters " as the Welsh. Professor Max Müller in his *"Chips," Vol. 3, p. 257,* writes—" It (the Cornish) seems to have been a melodious, and yet by no means an effeminate language, and Scawen places it in this respect above most of the Celtic dialects. 'Cornish,' he says, ' is not to be gutterally pronounced as the Welsh for the most part is, nor mutteringly as the Armorick, nor whiningly as the Irish (which two latter qualities seem to have been contracted from their servitude) but must be lively and manly spoken like other primitive tongues.' "

That Cornish should have died out sooner than its kindred Welsh or Armoric, although they are fast following its fate, is not surprising when the comparatively limited territory in which, and the smallness of the population among whom it obtained, are considered ; but other causes in its speedy disappearance as a living tongue may be found in the carelessness of the Cornish to resist Anglo-Saxon innovations, in this respect at least differing from their Welsh cousins, and to a neglect of the invention of printing, and the consequent non-existence of a church service, catechisms, &c., in the vulgar (Cornish) tongue, neither of which were so lost sight of in Brittany.

One would be sorry to see the old Mousehole fishwoman, Dolly Pentreath, altogether removed from the pedestal on which Mr. Daines Barrington placed her in 1768, as being " the last person who spoke Cornish fluently ;" but it is certain she was by no means the last. There is still extant a letter written in Cornish by a Mousehole fisherman in 1776, who says in it, that he learnt the language as a boy ; and that when at sea with his father and others he did not hear a word of English for a week together.* Cornish was understood and spoken by many on to the beginning of the present century. In 1790 according to Pryce, Cornish was still spoken in the West, and the Matthews' of Newlyn, one of whom died in 1800, are known to have spoken it more fluently than Dolly Pentreath. It lingers even now in a multitude of words commonly used by our agricultural labourers and fishermen ; I remember as a child myself being taught by tradition, orally of course, to count, and say the Lord's Prayer in Cornish, and I dare say there is many a youngster in Newlyn at the present moment who can score in Cornish as readily as he can in English.

Here are the numerals by way of comparison in

	WELSH,	CORNISH, AND	BREZONEC.
1	un	un or unan	unn or unan
2	daw *masc.*	dew *masc.*	daow *masc.*
,,	dwy *fem.*	dui *fem.*	diow *fem.*
3	tri *m.*	tri *m.*	tri *m.*
,,	tair *f.*	teir *f.*	teir *f.*
4	pedwar *m.*	peswar *m.*	pevar *m.*
,,	pedair *f.*	pedar *f.*	peder *f.*
5	pymp	pymp	pemp
6	chwêch	whêh	c'houec'h

*Quarterly Review, July, 1867, p. 40.

	WELSH,	CORNISH,	AND	BREZONEC.
7	saith	seyth		seiz
8	wyth	eyth		eiz
9	naw	naw		naô
10	dêg	dec		dek
11	un-ar-ddeg	unnec		unnek
12	deu-ddeg	dewthec		daouzek
13	tri-ar-ddeg	trithec		trizek
14	pedwar-ar-ddeg	peswarthec		pevarzek
15	pymtheg	pymthec		pemzek
16	un-ar-bymtheg	whêthec		c'houezek
17	dau-ar-bymtheg	seythec		seitek
18	tri-ar,bymtheg	eythec		triouec'h
,,	or dau naw			
19	pedwar-ar-bymtheg	nawnthec		naontek
20	ugain	ugans		uguent
30	deg-ar-hugain	dec warn ugans		dek war huguent
40	dew gain	dew ugans		daow uguent
50	{ deg-a'-deugain	hanter cans		hanter cant
	{ hanner cant			
100	cant	cans		cant

Please note how the Cornish steadily marches through the 'teens' without being like the Welsh reduced to express 19 by 15 + 4 and 2 × 9; or 18, by 3 × 6 as the Brezonec.

M

WELSH.	CORNISH.
From the Welsh Book of Common Prayer.	*In the orthography of the Cornish Drama, adapted from Williams' Gerlyver Cernewec.*

CREDO.

CREDO 'R APOSTOLION.	CREGYANS A'N ABESTELETH.
1. Credaf yn nuw Dad Holl-gyf-oethog, Creawdwr nef a daear :	1. Cresaf yn Dew an Tas Olgal-losec, gwrear a'n nef, ha'n nôr :
2. Ac yn Jesu Grist ei un Mab ef, ein Harglwydd ni ;	2. Hag yn Jhesu Gryst y yn mâb ef, agan Arluth ny ;
3. Yr hwn a gaed trwy yr Yspryd Glân, A aned o Fair Forwyn,	3. Nêb a ve deny thys dre an Spyrys Sans, genys a'n Werches Vary,
4. A ddïoddefodd dan Pontius Pilatus, a groeshoeliwyd, a fu farw, ac a gladdwyd ;	4. A wodhevys yn dan Pontius Pilatus, a ve crowsys, marow hag ancledys,
5. A ddisgynodd i uffern ; y trydydd dydd y cyfodd, o feirw ;	5. Ef a dhyescynnas the iffarn an tressa dyth ef a dhedhoras dheworth an marow ;
6. A esgynodd i'r nefoedd, Ac y mae yn eistedd ar ddeheulaw Dduw Dad Holl-gyfoethog ;	6. Hag a escynnas the'n nêf; hag yma ow sedhé war dorn dychow an Tas Olgallosec ;
7. Oddi yno y daw i farnu byw a meirw.	7. Alena ef a dhue the vrusy bew ha marow.
8. Credaf yn yr Yspryd Glân ;	8. Cresaf yn Spyrys Sans ;
9. Yr Eglwys Sân Gatholig ; Cummun y Saint ;	9. An Eglos Sans, dres an bys, cowethyans an Sansow ;
10. Maddeuant Pechodau ;	10. Dewyllans pechasow ;
11. Adgyfodiad y Cnawd,	Dedhoryans an corf ;
12. A'r Bywyd tragywyddol. Amen.	12. Ha'n bewnans hep dyweth. Amen.

CORNISH.	BREZONEC.
"As formerly used in all the Cornish Churches."— GILBERT. *Some words however seem doubtful.*	*From the "Catekismou Leon," published with authority of the Bishop of Kemper and Leon, 1865.*

CREDO.

CREGIANS A'N ABESTELY.	SYMBOLEN AN EBESTEL.
1. Me agris aez en Du, an Tas allogogack, wresser a heu hag doar,	1. Me agred e Doue an Tad oll-galloudec, Crouer d'an eê ha d'an douar ;
2. Hag en Jesu Chrest, ys nuell mab agan Arluth,	2. Hag e Jesus Christ he Vab unic, hon Antrou ;
3. Neb ve concevijis ryb an hairon Sperres, genjis ay an Voz Mareea,	3. Pehini zo bet concevet eus ar Speret-Santel, ganet gant ar Verc'hez glorius* Vari ;
4. Cothaff orthaff Pontius Pilat, ve crowsye, maraws hag bethens,	4. En deus gouzanvet dindan Ponç Pilat ; a zo bet crucifiet, maro ha sebeliet ;
5. Of deskynas en the Iffran hag an trysa journa ef sevye arte thort an maraws,	5. A zo bet diskennet d'an ifernou, ha ressuscitet an trede deiz a varo da veo ;
6. Ef askynnas en the neuf : hag setvah wor an dighow dorne ay Du, as Tas allogollogack,	6. A zo bet pignet en eêvou, hag azezet en tu deou da Zoue an Tad oll-galloudec ;
7. Ag en a ef fyth dos the judgge ar beaw hag an maraws.	7. Ac'hano e teui da varn ar re veo hag ar re varo.
8. Me agris an benegas spirres,	8. Me a gred er Speret-Santel ;
9. An Hairon Catholic Eglos, an Communion ay Sans.	9. An Ilis Santel catholic ; Communion ar Zent ;
10. An givyans ay peags.	10. Remission ar pec'hejou ;
11. An sevyans ay an corfe	11. Resurrection ar c'hic ;
12. Hag an bewe regnaveffere Amen.	12. Ar vuez eternel. Evellen bezet grêt.

* (Note ecclesiastical) Cool interpolation !

NAMES, SPELLING, &c.

To be able to spell correctly argues a writer of more or less education. Correct spelling is not without its inconveniences; but then, correct spelling should be regarded and used rather with the view of pointing out and sustaining the original or actual meaning of the word than as a guide to pronunciation. This, which holds true of all languages more or less, is especially the case with English, and as to Cornish names of persons and places, I think, with the learned author of " *The History of Polperro,*" *p.* 49, that on the whole, "the oral transmission of a name is generally to be trusted before documentary evidence." But caution must be used even here—"Mên an vawr"—*The big rock*—has been corrupted, both orally and in the Ordnance and other maps, into "Man of war rocks;" "Mên eglos"—*Church rock*—has degraded to "The manacles," and "Pen y cwm guîg" metamorphosed into "Penny come quick!" &c., &c.

Those connected with the Ordnance Surveys, and the good people who assisted the Tithe Commissioners to draw out the apportionments are responsible for the continuance of many an error of this nature. And this is the more to be regretted, because with a very little trouble they might have ascertained the real names, and stereotyped them as it were, whereas we now have over and over again unnecessary stumbling blocks opposing us in getting at the meaning of an old Cornish name, by the wild way in which we find it spelt in the public maps, &c. Thus in the Mullyon tithe apportionment, the word " carrag "—*a rock*—is spelt in no less than eight different ways; "gweal " —*a field*—shares the same fate; " lan mên hayl "—*a stony moor inclosure*— appears as "Lummun Hal ;" "Tal an vean"—*little hill*—as "Tallen Vaughen ;" and "Mên dour "—*watery stone*—as " Man down !" &c. The best method then of arriving at the meaning of any old Cornish name is, for the most part, to divest oneself as far as possible of any preconceived notions as to its spelling, and to take an opportunity of listening personally to the pronunciation of the word by the inhabitants. Few, I suppose, would follow in the wake of the wiseacre who took Polurrian, a cove, to be Bolerion, the headland of Ptolemy, and not many a stranger, unless he happen to be a Celt, would find it easy, even after having heard it from the mouth of a native, to give it the true pronunciation; but once thus having heard it, if you have any knowledge at all of the language, the true word and its meaning occur to you immediately,—Polyrhian—*boundary pool.* Should you desire any confirmation of the correctness of your rendering, visit the spot yourself, as I have done in almost every one of the cases given below, and see if it fits. Here in the case before us, down the length of the valley to the Cove's mouth and out beyond, you may trace the large vein of conglomerate—the boundary—which separates the slate on the North side from the hornblende on the South. It is almost needless to add that you are safer with natural peculiarities than with artificial, the former being less liable to change.

NAMES OF FARMS, TENEMENTS, FIELDS, &C., IN MULLYON.

As given in the Tithe Apportionment.	The true Cornish Spelling.	Signification.
NAFREGO, called also locally FRECAS	Lan frechiau	Fruit trees enclosure
Menewoon	Mên y gûn, or Men y gwon	Stony Down
Dormon Pla	Dôr mên plat, or Doar maen plat	Flatstone field
Park Wollas	Parc wollas	Lower field
TREMENHEHE	TRE MEN HYR	Long stone dwelling
Park an Hall	Parc an hâl, or hayl	The moor field
Geveladre	Gweal an drê	Homer field
Parketh	Parc eithin	Furze field
Park Blendw	?	?
Park en Venton	Parc an fenten	Spring, or well field
Gilley meadow	Celli	Grove
Redannack	Redanick	Ferny
MERES	MOR ROS	The sea valley
Enskellaw	Parc an scelli	The bat's field
Park Enshaft	Parc an sâf ty	Tree-stem hovel field
Dor Here	Dôr hyr	Long land

As given in the Tithe Appor-tionment.	The true Cornish Spelling.	Signification.
Park Landridge	Parc lan trig	Dwelling enclosure field
Morrop	Môr ryp	Beside the sea
The Reen	Ryne	The channel of a stream
SHETA	? SETHAR	Gulls' (abode)
LA FLOUDER	LAN FROWDIAU	Springs, or small water-falls enclosure
Belhere	? Beler	Watercress
Arrow	Garow	Rough (place)
Goss Gardens	Cors	Sedge
TREGELLES	TRE GOLLAS	Ruined dwelling
HALLAS VEAN	HAL GLAS VEAN	Little green moor
GWEELE AN CABBIN	GWEAL AN KE BIHAN	Little enclosed field
PARK VENTON SAH	PARC AN FENTEN SAW	Spring-in-the-cleft field
THE WEETH	GWYTH	The high, conspicuous place
TRENANCE VEAN	TRE NANS VEAN	Little dwelling in the valley
Bellurian	Pol yrhian	Boundary Pool
Park Jarne	Parc dzharn	Garden field
Crick Mawgan	Creeg môr gan	Stony mound by the sea
Park Shoel	Parc is hâl	Field below the moor
Pednan vounder	Pen an vounder	The head of the lane
Trenoweth	Tre nowyth	New dwelling
Meixers	?	
GREAT TRENANCE	TRE NANS VEUR, or VEOR	Great dwelling in the valley
Park Kistall	Parc castel	Castle field
Park Loar	Parc luar	Garden field
Tallen Vaughen	Tal an vean	Little hill-top
Park Emmet	?	
Park Mellon	Parc melin	Mill field
Crigg ear	Creegiau	Hillocks

As given in the Tithe Appor-tionment.	The true Cornish Spelling.	Signification.
GARRO	GAROW	Rough
Pearn Gweal	?	
Higher Keine	Cein	Ridge (of a hill)
Park Bush	Parc bôs, or bus	Fodder field
Park Creame	Parc grean	Gravel field
Park Mage	Parc mês	Plain, open field
Ghost field	Cors	Sedge
Park Jairn	Parc Dzharn	Garden field
ENNIS	ENYS	Island
Pasty Pans		
PREDANNACK WARTHA	PREDANICK WARTHA	Higher ferny (spot)
Croft an creeg	Croft an creeg	Stony mound croft
Burrow Croft	,,	,,
Cuckoo Rose	Côg y rôs	Cuckoo valley
Park Bean	Parc bihan, bean or vean	Little field
Park Mere	Parc meur, or veor	Big field
Davere	Dôr veor, or veur	Large land
Park menor	Parc mener, meneth	Mountain field
Dor Cairn	Dôr carn	Rocky land
Dor Couth	Dôr coth	Old land
Dor Woll	Dôr Wollas	Lower land
Goon Vean	Gûn Vean	Little down
Carne Lyer	Carn lyha, or leir	Smallest cairn
Vuldo	?	
Herlam	Hyr lan	Long enclosure
Well Gooth	Gweal coid	Plantation field
Lummun Hal	Lan mên hâl	Stony moor enclosure
Lana Mars	Lan an merch	Horses enclosure
Kullore	Cûl oar	Narrow land
* Gobben	Gobben	Fruitful

* The richest bit of ground on a farm is frequently termed "Gobben." The root is *"gober"* a reward, recompense, that which pays for cultivation.

As given in the Tithe Apportionment.	The true Cornish Spelling.	Signification.
Croft Noweth	Croft Nowyth	New Croft
Park Vro	Parc Vro, or Bro	Country field
Well Kerens	Gweal Cerynys	Dear, loved, field
Daroose	Dôr rôs	The valley land
Man down (!)	Mên dour	Watery stone
Gobben Higgo	Gobben ogo	Cave in the rich field
Park Hedrass	Parc an dreis	Bramble field
Shafty Croft	Sâf ty Croft	Tree-stem hovel field
Well Vrouse	Gweal brâs	Rich field
Sevan Park	Parc Sevi	Strawberry Park
Monop ? *Mosrop*	Môr ryp	By the sea
The Praze	Prâs	Meadow
Tregwinning	Tre gwenyn	Bees' abode
Bongey ? *Bougey*	Boudzhi	Cow-house
Barr Croft	Bar C.	Hilltop C.
Creigullow	Creeg culow	Rocky hilltops
Halkimbra	Hâl cymro	Briton's moor
Hewan ? *Hervan*	?	
TREVITHO	TRE BEDHOW	The place of graves
Geu Orchard	Ceow Orchard	Orchard fields
Park Woon	Parc gûn	Down, moor, field
Lapego ? Lafrego locally called Frecas	Lan frechiau	Fruit trees enclosure
Park Grosise	Parc crows ys	Under-cross field
Penhale	Pen hâl	Head of the moor
CLAHAR GARDEN	Cleyr carn	Bright rocks (heap of)
Park Hebye		
Park Hebyr		
Carrick Here	Carrag hyr	Long rock
Park Cairn	Parc carn	Rock (heap of) field
Park Vabyn		

As given in the Tithe Apportionment.	The true Cornish Spelling.	Signification.
St. Maloes Moor		
Sampson's Croft		
Cheponds	Tshyi, or chy pons	Bridge house
Chyponds	,,	,,
Remeal	Tre Mihal, or Maêl	Michæls' dwelling
Renuel		
Venton Vidon	? Fenten Fydhyn	The trusted well
Castle Cover	? gover	Rivulet
NEWTON	...	New Town—*Saxon*
Lean Loch	Lyn leauch	Calf's pool
TREWOON	TRE GÛN	Dwelling on the down
Har Strick	?	
Gual Dallar	Gweal dall	Blind field
Kin Her	Ceyn hyr	Long ridge
FENTON ARIANCE	FENTEN ARHANS	Silver well
VOUNDER	VOUNDER	The Lane
Park Grow	Parc grow	Gravel, or sandy field
Park Dray	Parc derow	Oaks' field
Park Dry	,,	,,
Tees	?	
MEAVER	MEA' VEOR	Great meadow
Park Parrack	? Parc prathac	Meadowy field
Karrack	Carrag	Rocks
Park an Joppa	?	
TREWITHNOE	TIRETH NOWYTH	New, or bare land
Park an leddan	Parc an ledan	The broad field
KYNANCE	KE' NANS	The shut in, enclosed valley
PRISKE	PRYSC	Underwood
Tubbon Vineyard	Tubn	A clod
Tretharrap Moor	?	
POLHORMON	POL OAR MEN	Earth stone pool

N

As given in the Tithe Apportionment.	The true Cornish Spelling.	Signification.
Calebna	Calenia	Wood dove's (abode)
Calebred	,,	,,
Bosweddaen for Rose-widden	Rôs gwydn	White valley
Park Scheta for Sheba	Parc sciber	Barn field
Loreer	Luar hyr	Long garden
ANGROWSE	AN CROWS	The Cross
Lenogar	Lan ogo	Cave enclosure
Park Bullas	Parc Pilez	Bare, bald field
Park Creaze	Parc crês	The middle, central field
Parc Scawen	Parc Scawen	Elder tree field
Dor Hare	Dor hyr	Long land
Sparnon	Spern gûn	Thorny down
Park Brougey	Parc Boudzhi	Cow house field
Park Wavan	Parc gwavan	Wintry field
Dor Main	Dôr myin	Stony land
Lidgia	Lidzhu	Ashes, remains of anything burnt
Crook Main	Cruc myin	Stony burrow, or mound
Park Minish	Parc minys	Little field
DOMAINE	DOR MYIN	Stony land
COLROGER	Col roger	Roger's ridge
TRESPRISEN	TRE SPRIDION	Spirit, or haunted dwelling
Park Crigar	Parc crigow	Hillocky field
Park Ebsar	?	
TERE BEAN	TYR BEAN	Small land
MEVER CREASE	MEAVEOR CRES	Middle Meaveor
Park Scheba	Parc sciber	Barn field
Park Nithen	Parc an eithin	Furzy field
Park Woon	Parc gûn	Down field
PREDANNACK WOLLAS	PREDANICK WOLLAS	Lower Predannack

As given in the Tithe Apportionment.	The true Cornish Spelling.	Signification.
Pedn menon	Pedn maen	Rocky head
Casky Lallah	? Coské le lowarn	Foxes' sleeping place
Park an Vave		
Dor Boobah	? Dôr boba	Blockhead's land
Penonack	Pen on ick	Ash tree head
Pentinick	Pen denick	Hilly head
Loga Stoggoth	Loga stoc coth	Heap of old tree trunks
Vea Ddan	?	
Venton Vyvyan	Fenten Vyvyan	Vyvyans well
Menor Gwidden	Mên y gwydn	White stone
Deager	? Dege'	Tenth, Tithe
Dearger		,,
Belowley	Pel lo le	Distant pool place
Vraddan	Bradn	Crow's or Choughs
Jolly Town	? Diawl Towan	Devil's Down

It will be seen that I am unable to interpret all these names, and some of the renderings are doubtful; but how full of poetry they, many of them, are! For example, 'Let us away by Le Flouder and Schetas to Polurrian and Pedn y Ke,' on past Carrag lûz, Porthmellin and the Vro to Creeg Morgan,' which fully rendered into English will run thus,—'Let us away by the water springs and the sea bird's home, on past the hoary rock, the mill cove and the brow, to the stony hillocks by the sea.'

NAMES OF HEADLANDS, COVES, &C.

As given in the Tithe Apportionment.	The true Cornish Spelling.	Signification.
Poljew	Pol du	Black pool
Many Grib	Mên y grîb	Rock like a comb
Menuel	Mên hewel	The conspicuous rock
Lew gabm	Lo cabm	Crooked pool

As given in the Tithe Apportionment.	The true Cornish Spelling.	Signification.
* Innis	Enys	The Island
Polglaze	Pol glâs	Green pool
Higgo mesul	Ogo ?	? Cave
Polbream	Pol bream	Bream (fish) pool
Polurrian	Pol yrhian	Edge, margin, boundary pool
Pedna Quay	Pedn y Ké	The enclosed head
Carrick gloose	Carrag lûz	The grey rock
Henscarth	Hen Scath	Old boat
Scorvan, the Ear	Scovarn	The ear (rock)
Porth Mellin	Porth Mellin	Mill Cove
Porpig	Porth Pyg, or Peg	Beak, or small cove
Vounder Nean	Vounder an Ean	Lamb's path
Innis Pruen	Enys Bronnow	The Island of round, breast like protuberances
Tregwin	Tre gwyn	The white spot
Tol dew	Tol du	Black hole
Lappen Kean	Ladn ceyn	Broad ridge, or head
† The Vroe	Vro, or Bro	The hill, brow, &c.
The Rinyard	Ryniau	Stream channels
The Chair		
Canavas	Ké nabos	‡ The hollow or bight of knowing, or by which you may know.
Main tail	Mên te heul	Sunny Rock
Pedn Predannack	Pen Predanick	Predannack Head
The Vradden	Bradn	The crows, or chough's rock

* Called also "Uncle Issy's garden," one Israel Odger having cultivated a small plot on the top of this rock some 150 years ago.

†* About 100 years ago, a man of the name of Uren climbed the Gull Rock without the aid of ropes, &c. He was ever afterwards called "Old Vro."

‡ "The tell tale bight." Our fishermen know by the appearance of the water in Canavas what is its state at their landing place in the Cove. If it be rough in Canavas, they will have rough landing at the Cove, and *vice versa.*

As given in the Tithe Apportionment.	The true Cornish Spelling,	Signification.
Park a bihan	Parc an vean, or byan	Little field
Ugethawr	Ogo dour	Watery cave
Polhorneck	Pol cornick	Corner pool
Georges Cove		
Vellan Head	Velen	Yellow
Pengersick	Pen corsick	Sedgy head
Gersick an awn	Gersick an awn	Sedgy river
Hugo pons	Ogo pons	Bridge cave
Gue Greze	Gew corez, or cors	Sedgy valley
Pigeon Hugo	Bigeon, or Poethon ogo	Dirty, or boiling cave
The Horse	An ors	The bear
The Pound		
The Rill		
Par an oel	Parc an heul	Sunny sand
Kynance	Kénans	The enclosed or hedged-in valley

Here are a few names of places in Mullyon strung together after the manner of the late Rev. Le Grice's "Lappior Jem," who is represented as singing to his companion "Shalal-a-shackets," a somewhat similar strain commencing :—

Vel-an-drakya, Cracka, Cudner
Truzmenhale, Chûn, Crowz an wra, &c.

NOMINA MULLYONIANA.

Mullyon, Dor mên Plat, Nafrego
Mên y gwiddn, Loar, Vea Ddan
Troon Halkymbro, Gobben Huggo
Gweal an Cabbin, Vro, Vraddan.

Lana Mars, Jarine, Gual Dallah
Venton Vyvyan, Park Wavan
Gew, Calebna, Casky Lallah
Pedn an Vounder, Creeg Mawgan.

Logga Stoggoth, Pradannack wartha,
Vuldo, Lidgia, Polurrian,
Parc an Venton Sah, Dor Boobah,
Praze, Grosize, Chypons, Sevan.

Most persons east of the Tamar might easily suppose this to be "Persian" or any other language.

EXTRACTS FROM THE REGISTER OF BURIALS, MULLYON.

URIALS in Mullyon Churchyard during a period of 50 years, viz.:—
from 1 January, 1813 to 31 December, 1862, inclusive.

Under the age of 5 years	...	...	...	...	148
Between 5 years old and 10	...	...	25
,,	10	,,	15	... ...	19
,,	15	,,	20	... ...	22
,,	20	,,	25	... ...	39
,,	25	,,	30	... ...	14
,,	30	,,	35	... ...	23
,,	35	,,	40	... ...	15
,,	40	,,	45	... ...	20
,,	45	,,	50	... ...	21
,,	50	,,	55	... ...	15
,,	55	,,	60	... ...	28
,,	60	,,	65	... ...	31
,,	65	,,	70	... ...	35
,,	70	,,	75	... ...	46
,,	75	,,	80	... ...	48
,,	80	,,	85	... ...	39
,,	85	,,	90	... ...	29
,,	90	,,	95	... ...	14
,,	95	,,	100	... ...	2

And there were 20 buried whose ages were not known.

It will be seen then that the *greater number* of persons (exclusive of infants under 5 years old) dying in that 50 years, attained the age of 75 and upwards ; the next greatest number reached 70 and upwards, and the next 80 and upwards.   The same number as this last died between 20 and 25, and the next largest number lived to between 85 and 90 years.

I have made similar computations for the same period of years from the register books of the other parishes in Meneag, but none shew so lengthy an average life as this of the parishioners of Mullyon.   In 1873 I buried an old lady who before she died declared she had reached the advanced age of 101. Her baptismal certificate proves her to have been at least 99 when she died.

The population of Mullyon in 1861 was 679.

The total number of burials in 50 years, 653.

Between 3rd September, 1868 and 26th September, 1869 there was, besides that of an infant of three weeks old, but one death in the parish.

Of the different portions of the year the month of May would seem to be the most fatal at Mullyon, April, February, March, January, December, June, October, July, September following in the order given, while August and November are the healthiest.

RUINS OF ANCIENT CHAPEL ON CLAHAR-GARDEN ESTATE, MULLYON.

From a sketch by the Author.

APPENDIX A.

PEDIGREES, HISTORICAL JOTTINGS, &c.

Inquisitio [1] post mortem at Truro, 16th September, 8th Henry VI (1429) on John Petyt, armiger, who held in the manor of Predannack Wartha by gift of John Petyt, late lord of Trenerth, knight, &c., &c. . . . . Said John died 23rd July, and John Petyt, the son, was aged 30.

Inquisit. Bk. of Henry VI, John Petyt held Predannek, formerly held by the Bishop of Exeter.

Inquisit. post mort. 28th October, 34 Henry VI, (1455) on John Petyt, armiger. Said John held parcel of manor of Predannack Wartha by gift of John Petyt, knight, late lord of Trenerth, to Michæl Petyt and Amicia his wife, &c., of whom said John in writ named was heir, viz. : the son of John, the son of said Michæl and Amicia, held of the King *in puro socagio* as of his castle of Launceston, as of Duchy of Cornwall, &c. . . . . Said John died 10th June, and John his son was then aged 28 years and more.

Ped : Fin : 17 Edward I, No. 6, Michæl le Petyt, Qu : John le Petyt, def : lands in Trenerth, Predanek wartha, &c.

In the year 1297, King Edward I imprisoned many of the Cornish clergy at Launceston, for refusing to pay the taxes. This refusal was made on the strength of the famous Bull of Pope Boniface VIII—"Clerices laicos "—which forbad the taxation of the clergy. Among those thus imprisoned was John le Petit, parson of the Church of S. Melan in Kirrier.[2]

---

1 Harleian Society Ed. of Heraldic Visit : of Cornwall in 1620, Ed : by Drake and Vivian.
2 Prynne, Records pp. 700 and 713.

O

TABLE I.

PEDIGREE OF LE PETYT.

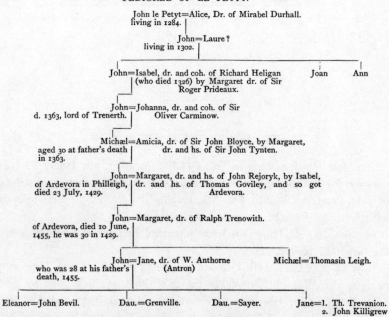

John le Petyt=Alice, Dr. of Mirabel Durhall.
living in 1284.

John=Laure?
living in 1302.

John=Isabel, dr. and coh. of Richard Heligan   Joan   Ann
(who died 1326) by Margaret dr. of Sir
Roger Prideaux.

John=Johanna, dr. and coh. of Sir
d. 1363, lord of Trenerth.   Oliver Carminow.

Michæl=Amicia, dr. of Sir John Bloyce, by Margaret,
aged 30 at father's death   dr. and hs. of Sir John Tynten.
in 1363.

John=Margaret, dr. and hs. of John Rejoryk, by Isabel,
of Ardevora in Philleigh,   dr. and hs. of Thomas Goviley, and so got
died 23 July, 1429.   Ardevora.

John=Margaret, dr. of Ralph Trenowith.
of Ardevora, died 10 June,
1455, he was 30 in 1429.

John=Jane, dr. of W. Anthorne   Michæl=Thomasin Leigh.
who was 28 at his father's   (Antron)
death, 1455.

Eleanor=John Bevil.   Dau.=Grenville.   Dau.=Sayer.   Jane=1. Th. Trevanion.
                                                                  2. John Killigrew

Decanus et capitulum ecclesiæ beati Petri, Exon. : finem fecerunt cum Rege per vigenti libras pro licentiâ ingrediendi unam acram terræ in Rossewyk in Pengarreg et advocationem ecclesiæ Sancti Melani in Kirrier et pro licentiâ appropriandi ecclesiam antedictam "[1] Rossewyk *(Rôs gwic)* is the manor extending over Landewednack, Ruan Minor, and Grade. [2]

" De nonâ garbarum vellerum et agnorum parochiæ ecclesiae Sancti Melani taxata ad VIII libras et sic rendita Johanni Rous, Nicholas Rogers, Roger Trenans et Johanni Petit, De quintadecima vero nihil."[3]

---

1 Rotularum Orig : Abb : (Exchequer) I, p. 171.

2 Davies Gilbert, II, p. 358.

3 Inquisitiones nonarum (*i.e.*, the ninth sheaf, lamb and fleece granted to Edward III for the war in 1340), p. 343.

Of neighbouring parishes Grade paid £3, the two Ruans and Gunwalloe £4 3s. 4d. each, &c.

The John Petit here mentioned is Sir John, who married Johanna, daughter of Sir Oliver Carminow, and who died 1363.

TABLE II.

PEDIGREE OF DE CERISIS, DE CERISEAUX, SERJEAULX, SERGEAUX OF PRADANNACK IN MULLYON, COLQUITE IN S. MABYN, KILLIGARTH IN TALLAND.

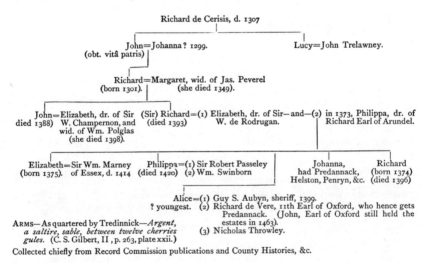

Richard de Cerisis, d. 1307

John═Johanna? 1299.
(obt. vitâ patris)

Lucy═John Trelawney.

Richard═Margaret, wid. of Jas. Peverel
(born 1301). (she died 1349).

John═Elizabeth, dr. of Sir   (Sir) Richard═(1) Elizabeth, dr. of Sir—and—(2) in 1373, Philippa, dr. of
died 1388) W. Champernon, and   (died 1393)   W. de Rodrugan.   Richard Earl of Arundel.
      wid. of Wm. Polglas
      (she died 1398).

Elizabeth═Sir Wm. Marney   Philippa═(1) Sir Robert Passeley   Johanna,   Richard
(born 1375). of Essex, d. 1414   (died 1420) (2) Wm. Swinborn   had Predannack,   (born 1374)
                                                             Helston, Penryn, &c. (died 1396)

Alice═(1) Guy S. Aubyn, sheriff, 1399.
? youngest. (2) Richard de Vere, 11th Earl of Oxford, who hence gets
             Predannack. (John, Earl of Oxford still held the
             estates in 1463).
ARMS—As quartered by Tredinnick—*Argent,*   (3) Nicholas Throwley.
a saltire, sable, between twelve cherries
gules. (C. S. Gilbert, II , p. 263, plate xxii.)

Collected chiefly from Record Commission publications and County Histories, &c.

TABLE III.

PEDIGREE OF KEMPTHORNE.

The family name, which was anciently written Ley, originated from an estate so called in the parish of Beer Ferrers, in Devon. In the reign of Edward III, a younger son of Ley, of Ley, seated himself at Kempthorne, in the parish of Clawton near Holdsworthy, and so became designated by the name of Kempthorne, *alias* Ley. From this house descended John Kempthorne *alias* Ley, of Tonacombe (1) in Moorwinstow. A younger branch of the family settled in Mullyon, as will be seen from the extracts given below from the Registers of this parish. The Kempthornes have long possessed several good estates, and have furnished the British navy with some excellent officers.

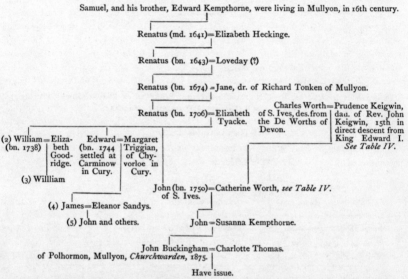

Samuel, and his brother, Edward Kempthorne, were living in Mullyon, in 16th century.

Renatus (md. 1641)=Elizabeth Heckinge.

Renatus (bn. 1643)=Loveday (?)

Renatus (bn. 1674) =Jane, dr. of Richard Tonken of Mullyon.

Renatus (bn. 1706)=Elizabeth Tyacke.

Charles Worth=Prudence Keigwin, of S. Ives, des. from the De Worths of Devon. dau. of Rev. John Keigwin, 15th in direct descent from King Edward I. *See Table IV.*

(2) William=Eliza-(bn. 1738) beth Goodridge.

(3) Willliam

Edward=Margaret (bn. 1744 settled at Carminow in Cury. Triggian, of Chyvorloe in Cury.

(4) James=Eleanor Sandys.

(5) John and others.

John (bn. 1750)=Catherine Worth, *see Table IV.* of S. Ives.

John=Susanna Kempthorne.

John Buckingham=Charlotte Thomas. of Polhormon, Mullyon, *Churchwarden*, 1875.

Have issue.

ARMS—Ley and Kempthorne quarterly.—Ley, *Three lions' heads proper, with chevron noir on a field argent.* Kempthorne, *Three thorn trees proper, on a field argent.*
CREST—*Dove with olive branch, A Lion sejant.*
MOTTO—Ley, "*Vicendo Victus*;" Kempthorne, "*Karenza whelas Karenza.*"

Collected from Gilbert's Historical Survey of Cornwall, the Mullyon Registers, &c.

NOTES TO TABLE III.

(1). From Tonacombe house descended John Kempthorne, Attorney-at-law and horse officer in the service of Charles I. His youngest son, John, entered the navy and became a very successful commander, and was particularly victorious in his engagements with the Corsairs of Algiers, and for his valour and conduct therein he received the honour of Knighthood from Charles II, 30th April, 1670. After many great and important services, he successfully rose to the rank of rear-admiral of the red and vice-admiral of the blue, and on 26th November, 1675, was appointed Commissioner of the Navy at Portsmouth, where he died 19th October, 1679.

A monument to his memory is erected in the N. Aisle of Portsmouth Church. His son Morgan Kempthorne increased the naval splendour, which his father had began in the service of his country. He served as Lieutenant in the Mary Rose, of which his father was Captain in 1671. In 1679, he was appointed Commander of the Kingfisher, and was sent immediately afterwards to the Mediterranean with a convoy, where he remained till he met his death in 1681

EXTRACT OF A LETTER FROM NAPLES, MAY 24TH, 1681.

"Here is now in port an English Frigate, called the King's Fisher, lately commanded by Captain Kempthorne, who maintained a fight with seven Algerines, Men of War, with so much bravery and courage, that the people here are in admiration of it, and with great curiosity flock to see the ship and men, who behaved themselves with so much extraordinary courage and resolution. The account that we have of the action is, that on Sunday last, about one of the clock, they made eight sail, that soon after they discovered that they were seven Turks, Men of War, and a small Saltea, and being come within pistol shot, the first of the Algerines poured into them his broadside and small shot, and then sprung his Luff and stood off to give way to the second; who also coming as near, did the like, and then gave place to the third, who having given the like salute, made way for the Admiral, the King's Fisher very warmly answering them with her great and small shot. Here Captain Kempthorne was wounded in the hand, and at the same time, part of his belly taken away by a cannon bullett, of which in a few minutes after he died, to the great trouble of the whole ship's company, who could not but be concerned at the loss of so brave a Commander."

FROM GILBERT; SEE *Biog: Naval:* VOL. I, p. 397.

(2). William Kempthorne, born at Tremenhee, entered the navy as midshipman on board the Macclesfield. In 1777, he was opposed off Barbadoes, in His Majesty's packet Granville, to three American privateers, two of whom were each of equal force to the Granville, and lay alongside her in a raking position. After a desperate action, in which Captain Kempthorne received a severe wound in his head and lost the roof of his mouth, the enemy was compelled to sheer off, and the Granville and her brave commander returned to England. In 1792, he commanded the Antelope packet, and died of a fever as he was returning from Halifax.

(3). William, eldest son of the above, entered the navy under the patronage of Sir Edwd. Pellew, whom, after various encounters on the French coasts, he accompanied to the East Indies. Here he was appointed to the command of the Diana, brig of 8 guns. Afterwards he was appointed to the Belzebub, and commanded the division of bomb vessels on the ever memorable attack on Algiers, and for the gallantry which he displayed on this occasion he was promoted to the rank of Post Captain.

(4). James Kempthorne, who also entered the navy, accompanied the gallant Boscawen in many of his daring enterprizes, and ultimately attained the rank of British Admiral.

(5). John, eldest son of the above James Kempthorne, was educated St. John's College, Cambridge, and at the age of 21, became Senior Wrangler and Fellow of his College.

TABLE IV.

EDWARD I, KING OF ENGLAND, d. 1307=Eleanor, dr. of Ferdinand III, King of Castille.

Princess Elizabeth Plantagenet, d. 1316=Humphrey de Bohun, Earl of Hereford and Essex.

Lady Margaret de Bohun, d. 1391 Hugh de Courtenay, Earl of Devon.

Lady Margaret de Courtenay, d. 1392 Theobald Granville, Esq., descended from Rollo.

Willm. Granville, Esq., of Stowe, Cornwall, Philippa, dr. of Willm. Lord Bonville, K.G.
d. abt. 1450.

Sir Thos. Granville, Knt., High Sheriff of Cornwall,=Elizabeth, sister of Sir Theobald Gorges, Knt.
d. 1483.

Sir Thos. Granville, Knt., K.B., d. abt. 6 Hen. VIII=Isabel, dr. of Sir Oates Gilbert, Kt., of Compton, Devon

Roger Granville, Esq., Sheriff of Cornwall, d. 1524 Margaret, dr. of Richard Whitley, Esq., of Efford.

Sir Richard Granville, Kt., Sheriff of Devon, d. 1552=Matilda, dr. of John Beville, Esq., of Gwarnock,
Cornwall.

Mary Granville=John Giffard, Esq., of Brightly, Devon.

John Giffard, Esq., of Brightley, Devon=Honor, dr. of Walter Erle, Esq., of Charborough,
Dorset.

Arthur Giffard, Esq., of Brightley, Devon=Anne, dr. of Thos. Leigh, Esq., of Borough, Devon.

Colonel John Giffard, of Brightley, d. 1666=Joan, dr. of Sir John Wyndham, Knt., of Somerset.

Margaret Giffard, d. 1739=John Keigwin, Esq., of Mousehole, Cornwall.

Rev. John Keigwin, Vicar of Landrake and S. Erney,=Prudence, dr. of John Busvargus, Esq., of Busvargus,
Cornwall.   Cornwall.

Prudence Keigwin=Charles Worth, Esq., of S. Ives, Cornwall.

Extracted by Horace Pearce,
Esq., F.G.S.   Catherine Worth=John Kempthorne, of S. Ives, Cornwall.

TABLE V.

PEDIGREE OF TONKEN.

Tonken, Tonkin, formerly of Trevaunance in S. Agnes, trace back to the time of Richard II. John Tonken, of Trevaunance, in 1632 laid the foundation of a pier and fishing cove on his own estate. His grandson, Hugh, was sheriff of Cornwall in 1702; the male line of this branch became extinct in the 18th century.

There was also a family of Tonken resident in S. Keverne, which married an heiress of Brabin, and with whom probably the Tonkens of Mullyon were connected. The name first occurs in the Mullyon Registers on the burial of Paskua, the wife of Thomas Tonkin, of Trenance, in 1610. In 1618 Richard, son of John Tonkin is baptised, in 1670 John Kempthorne marries Jane Tonken, and in 1714 William Tonken marries Jane Kempthorne. Hugh, the vicar, held Trenance 1726 and onwards.

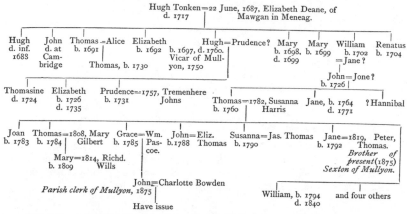

(*It is curious to note that the present* (1875) *Parish Clerk, the Churchwarden, and the Sexton of Mullyon are each allied to Hugh Tonken, the former Vicar.*)

Extracted from the Mullyon Registers, &c.

APPENDIX B.

EXTRACTS FROM CHURCHWARDEN'S BOOKS.

		s.	d.
1794-5.	To expence on Victory over the French	10	6
	(This was Earl Howe's Victory in the West Indies).		
1797.	To a distressed Sailor	2	6
1797-8.	To a form of Prayer or Thanksgiving for Signal Victory obtained over the Dutch Fleet by Admiral Duncan the 11th October last (Camperdown)	2	0
1798.	To a distressed Soldier	2	6

		s.	d.
1798-9.	To a rejoicing for a Victory obtained over the French Fleet by Admiral Nelson (Nile)	10	6
1800-1.	To forms of Prayer on the preservation of the King	2	0
	To a proclamation concerning the Corn	2	0
1802-3.	To a warrant to call fourth the boys for breaking the Church Windows	2	0
1803-4.	To a thanksgiving for the preservation of His Majesty from assassination	2	0
1804.	To a journey to Helston with a cart for healing (hellan) stone, but disapointed	6	6
1824.	To a letter from the High Priest	1	6

(There is an *Arch* Priest in this Diocese, to wit of Haccombe, Newton Abbot, whatever may be his peculiar functions or privileges; but "High Priest?" Is he the Bishop or the non-resident Vicar, or what?)

| 1831. | To Cushions for the Communion Altar | 11 | 6 |

(Here is a new term for ecclesiologists).

From 1786 to 1850.

Paid for 243 Foxes	£26	9	6
,, 3 Otters	0	3	0
,, 1 Badger	0	1	0
	£26	13	6

The last Fox paid for was in 1856 .... 1 6

There was a payment of 8s. 6d. made to the ringers on 29th May and on 4th November yearly, from 1785 to 1816, inclusive. The former evidently King Charles II and the Oak-day. But why on 4th November. The 6th November is our parish feast; was it on account of the landing of Prince William of Orange, in Torbay, 4th November, 1688?

APPENDIX C.

TELEGRAPHIC EXTENSION.

The following memorial was forwarded in May, 1873, to the Post Master General, having been signed by the Vicar and the principal inhabitants of Mullyon; by the Mayor, Aldermen, Town Councillors, Bankers, Ship Agents, and principal merchants of Penzance; by the Mayor and Council, Ship Agents, &c., &c., at Falmouth; by Lord Robartes; by the Commanding Inspectors of Coastguard at Falmouth, accompanied by letters of recommendation from the Secretaries of Lloyds, the R.N. Lifeboat Institution, &c., &c. :—

To the Right Honourable William Monsell, Post Master General,

Sir,

We, the undersigned inhabitants of Mullyon and others, believing that the extension of Telegraphic communication to this place would be productive of great public benefit, beg respectfully to submit to your consideration the following circumstances.

1. That Mullyon is situated on the eastern coast of Mount's Bay and is distant 7 miles from the nearest post-town—viz., Helston—and 5 miles from the nearest Telegraph Station—viz., Lizard.

2. That during the storms that are so prevalent here in the winter months, and which are so often fraught with loss of life and property, it is of the highest importance that Mullyon should be connected with the sea-ports, whence the assistance of steam power might be obtained in cases of emergency, as well as with other parts of the kingdom.

N.B.—In the last 6¼ years there have been 9 wrecks with a loss of 69 lives under Mullyon cliffs, on a bit of coast line not more than a mile and half in length, and in the last 10¼ years there have been 16 wrecks with loss of 90 lives on about 3 miles of coast.

3. That during the prevalence of easterly gales, a number of wind bound vessels, as many as 250 to 300, take up anchorage in Mullyon Roads; sometimes a large number of vessels are thus detained for from 7 to 21 days. The Captains of these vessels would gladly avail themselves of the Telegraph were there a station at Mullyon, instead of sending special messengers to a distance; and others, under similar circumstances, would doubtless call in here for orders rather than risk the delay or even danger of attempting to get further up channel.

4. That in addition to the convenience which would be afforded to the inhabitants generally, as well as to the numerous sea side visitors in the summer months, the proprietors of the important fishery off the coast would be greatly accommodated by the use of the Telegraph, since by its aid, fish which are now often lost would be secured at once, landed, and taken away.

5. That Telegraphic communication having already been established at the Lizard, the first outlay of the extension to Mullyon would be very trifling, since but 1¼ miles of posts and about 6 miles of wire would be required to connect Mullyon with that Station.

[Then follow the signatures.]

The response to the memorial was as follows :—

General Post Office, London,

16th June, 1873.

Telegraphs,

Sir,—In reply to your letter forwarding a memorial on behalf of the inhabitants of Mullyon, in regard to the establishment of a Postal Telegraph Office at that place, I beg leave to inform you that the department is not at the present time in a position to undertake any new engineering works.

I am, Sir, your obedient Servant,

F. J. SCUDAMORE.

A second and similar application was made through the instrumentality of John Tremayne, Esq., M.P., in April, 1875, with what result the following letter will shew :—

General Post Office, London,

24th May, 1875.

Telegraphs.

Sir,—In reply to your letter of the 12th ultimo, I am directed by the Post Master General to inform you that his Lordship has caused the application for an extension of the Postal Telegraph System to Mullyon to be very carefully considered, and I am to express his regret that having compared the expense which would be incurred in effecting and maintaining the extension and in providing for telegraph business at the Postal Telegraph Office sought to be established with the revenue likely to be earned, he is not prepared to entertain the application favorably.

I am, Sir, your obedient Servant,

F. J. SCUDAMORE.

APPENDIX D.

READINGS OF THE THERMOMETER, DURING FIVE YEARS, AT CHURCH TOWN, MULLYON, BEING ABOUT 200 FEET ABOVE SEA LEVEL.

1869.

THERMOMETRICAL READINGS TAKEN AT 9 A.M.

	Highest.	Lowest.	Average.	Range.
January	59	31	41	28
February	52	34	47	18
March	50	30	41	20
April	58	40	52	18
May	65	50	56	15
June	70	58	63	12
July	76	65	67	11
August	70	59	64	11
September	65	52	63	13
October	61	39	49	22
November	55	34	45	21
December	48	23	40	25

Highest reading for the year 76°—lowest 23°.

Mean average for the year at 9 o'clock, a.m., 52°.

1870.

THERMOMETRICAL READINGS TAKEN AT 9 A.M.

	Highest.	Lowest.	Average.	Range.
January	49	28	41	21
February	47	25	38	22
March	53	35	42	18
April	58	40	49	18
May	67	52	57	15
June	71	62	65	9
July	73	62	67	11
August	71	55	63	16
September	66	55	59	11
October	58	41	53	17
November	47	36	41	11
December	47	24	36	13

Highest reading for the year 73'—lowest 24°.

Mean average for the year at 9 o'clock, a.m., 51°.

1871.

THERMOMETRICAL READINGS TAKEN AT 9 A.M.

	Highest.	Lowest.	Average.	Range.
January	44	25	36	19
February	50	34	44	16
March	54	37	45	17
April	57	42	51	15
May	65	51	51	14
June	70	54	63	16
July	73	60	65	13
August	72	59	65	13
September	67	50	58	17
October	58	45	52	13
November	51	32	40	19
December	47	29	39	18

Highest reading for the year 73°—lowest 25°.

Mean average for the year at 9 o'clock, a.m., 51°.

1872.
THERMOMETRICAL READINGS TAKEN AT 9 A.M.

	Highest.	Lowest.	Average.	Range.
January	50	33	43	17
February	50	42	45	8
March	53	34	46	19
April	56	42	49	14
May	66	49	57	17
June	75	56	63	19
July	75	61	68	14
August	71	59	65	12
September	66	47	60	19
October	58	41	49	17
November	55	35	44	20
December	50	35	44	15

Highest reading for the year 75°—lowest 33°.

Mean average for the year at 9 o'clock, a.m., 52°.

1873.
THERMOMETRICAL READINGS TAKEN AT 9 A.M.

	Highest.	Lowest.	Average.	Range.
January	48	33	43	15
February	48	31	38	17
March	52	34	44	18
April	60	50	51	10
May	66	52	57	14
June	73	62	66	11
July	73	62	67	11
August	71	61	64	10
September	62	53	58	9
October	62	34	50	28
November	56	37	43	19
December	49	34	43	15

Highest reading for the year 73°—lowest 31°.

Mean average for the year at 9 o'clock a.m., 52°.

APPENDIX E.

The accommodation that is at present offered to visitors at Mullyon is not extensive. A few good lodging houses would answer well : for independently of its own attractions Mullyon is, from its central position, from the variety of its land and sea views, and for many other reasons, by far the best spot to select as head quarters for any persons intending to visit the whole of Menêag district. What we have, however, is unexceptionable. There is the " King's Arms," a respectable inn, situated in the Church Town, of which Mrs. Williams is the landlady ; and the " Old Inn " on the north-western skirts of the village, kept by Miss Mary Mundy.

I select the following extracts from the Visitors' Book of the latter, as being " most refreshing strains after the usual balderdash of would-be wits " that is commonly found in such chronicles :—

I

" Hospitium mundus tenet hospes munda magistra
Munditia floret sic vetus illa domus."

8:10:70.

2

" Infelix virgo, cui nomen Fata dederunt
' Munda ' malis scribis quam maculare licet
Omnia munda tuam circumdant undique sedem
Rident munditiis æquora, terra. polus.
At venit huc nemo qui chartam linguere mundam,
Sic Pollet nomen, munda puella potest."

20:4:74.

3

LAUDES HOSPITII VETERIS ET DOMINÆ MARIÆ MUNDÆ.

Full many bright things on this earth there be,
Which a pious man may enjoy with glee
    On Saturday or Sunday ;
But the brightest thing that chanced to me,
In Cornish land, was when I did see
    The " Old Inn," by Mary Mundy.

'Twas on Saturday afternoon
That I was trudging, a weary loon,
    To spend at the Lizard my Sunday,
When thro' the corner of my right eye,
The happy sign I did espy,—
    " OLD INN, by MARY MUNDY."

So I went in, and out came she,
With a face from which blue devils would flee
    On Saturday or on Sunday :
And I said as soon as I saw her face,
" I could not be housed in a better place,
    So I'll just stay here till Monday."

Quoth I, " Could you give me a dinner well spread,—
An old arm chair, and a well-air'd bed,—
    And a good short sermon on Sunday ?"
Quoth she, " Indeed, Sir, that we can,
For I guess no doubt you're a gentleman,
    As sure as my name is Mundy."

I went upstairs with a bound and a hop,
And I looked around the tight little shop,
    And I said, " Miss Mary Mundy !
There's not in London a grand hotel
Where, with such comfort, I could dwell,
    As with you, my dear Miss Mundy ! "

" You've got the tongue of a gentleman,"
Quoth she, " I do the best I can
    On Saturday or on Sunday."
" That's just the thing we all should do ;
But they who do it are few, and you
    Are one of the few, Miss Mundy ! "

But now to tell the feast she spread,
And with what delicate zest we fed
    On the day before the Sunday,
Would stagger the muse of a Tennyson,
And bring from the devil a benison
    On the head of Mary Mundy.

A London alderman, sleek and fat,
Would sigh for the sight of a duck like that
    Was served to us by Mundy,—
A roasted duck, with fresh green peas,
A gooseberry pie, and a Cheddar cheese,—
    A feast for a god on Sunday.

But the top of her skill I well may deem
Was the dear delight of the Cornish cream,—
    Both Saturday and Sunday,—
That down my throat did gently glide,
Like sweet Bellini's tuneful tide,
    By the liberal grace of Mundy.

And then to crown the banquet rare,
A brandy bottle she did bear,—
    (God bless thee ! Mary Mundy !)
And said, " Full sure a gentleman
Abhors the lean teetotal plan
    On Saturday or Sunday."

And when my weary frame did glow
With genial warmth from top to toe,
    (Good night ! my dear Miss Mundy,)
I slept on bed as clean and sweet
As lass that goes so trim and neat
    With her lover to Church on Sunday.

M—J

But why should I go on to sin,
Spinning bad rhymes to the good OLD INN
   While the bell is tolling on Sunday;
I'll go and hear short sermon there,—
Tho' the best of all sermons I declare
   Is the face of Miss Mary Mundy.

And I advise you all to hold
By the well-tried things that are good and old,
   Like this snug house of Mundy,—
The good OLD CHURCH and the good OLD INN;
And the old way to depart from sin,
   By going to Church on Sunday.

And if there be on Cornish cliffs
To swell his lungs with breezy whiffs
   Who can spare but only one day,
Let him spend it here,—and understand
That the brightest thing in the Cornish land
   Is the face of Miss Mary Mundy.

                     23:6:72.

Τοὺς στίχους τούτους συνεκάττυσε Ιωαννης Ὀικονόμος
Μελανίοκος, ἀνὴρ Καληδόνιος, θαυμαζων τὴν τε πάνυ
θειαν ἀρητὴν τὴν τῆς παρθενου Μούνδης, και τὴν του
πανδοχείου τούτου ἀσπιλον κομψότητα, τη ἡμέρα του
μηνος Ιουνις τρίτῃ επι τοις ἔικοσι ἔτει της ἐνσάρκου
ὀικονομίας ᾳ ω ζ β.

INDEX.

LIST OF SUBSCRIBERS.

THE RIGHT HONOURABLE LORD ROBARTES .. .. 4 copies.
THE RIGHT HONOURABLE VISCOUNT FALMOUTH.
THE RIGHT HONOURABLE EARL MOUNT EDGCUMBE.
THE RIGHT HONOURABLE LORD ELIOT.
THE RIGHT REVEREND THE LORD BISHOP OF EXETER .. 4 copies.
THE RIGHT REVEREND THE LORD BISHOP OF WINCHESTER.. 4 copies.
THE VERY REVEREND THE DEAN OF EXETER.
THE VENERABLE THE ARCHDEACON OF CORNWALL.
SIR RICHARD R. VYVYAN, BART., Trelowarren.
SIR JOHN ST. AUBYN, BART., M.P.
JOHN TREMAYNE, ESQ., M.P.
A. YOUNG, ESQ., M.P.
THE REVEREND PREBENDARY R. H. BARNES.
THE REVEREND PREBENDARY R. W. BARNES .. .. .. 2 copies.
THE REVEREND PREBENDARY HEDGELAND.
THE REVEREND DR. CAMPION, Queens' College, Cambridge .. 2 copies.
THE REVEREND C. W. BOASE, Exeter College, Oxford.
PROFESSOR J. S. BLACKIE, University of Edinburgh.
PROFESSOR LEONARD H. COURTENAY. Lincoln's Inn .. .. 2 copies.

Anderton, E. D., *Falmouth.*	Bolitho, T. S., *Penzance.*
Aston, Mrs.	Bolitho, W., Jun. „
St. Aubyn, Rev. A. H. Molesworth, *Clowance.*	Borlase, Rev. W.
Bancks, Joseph, *Broxbourne.*	Borrow, H., *Truro* .. .. 4 copies.
Barham, Charles, M.D., *Truro.*	Borrow, Rev. H. J. .. .. 2 copies.
Batten, Edward, *Penzance.*	Brinton, Geo., *Southampton* .. 4 copies.
Babbage, W. P., *Truro.*	Britton, Rev. T. H.
Beaton, J., *Tring.*	Broad, R. R., Sen., *Falmouth.*
Berry, Rev. A.	Broad, W., „
Berry, J., *London.*	Brougham, Rev. M. N.
Betts, Miss Annie.	Burch, Arthur, *Exeter.*
Blackwell, Miss, *Richmond.*	Bull, *Lieut.-Col.*
Bloxsome, Rev. W. H.	Bullocke, Rev. H., Jun.
Bloxsome, John, *Dursley.*	Bullocke, Gustavus.
Boaden, Thomas, *Cury.*	Caldwell, James, *Dumbarton.*
Boase, George, *London.*	Carus-Wilson, E. S., *Penmount* .... 2 copies.
Bolitho, J. Bedford, *Penzance.*	Carlyon, Rev. C. W.

Carlyon, E. T., *Truro*.
Carlyon, John,　　　,,
Chappell, Rev. W. P.
Chilcott, J. G., *Truro*.
Church, Rev. G. L.
Christoe, W. H., *Truro*.
Clapin, Rev. A. C.
Clough, C. B., *Chester*.
Cock, F. H., *Truro* .. .. 2 *copies*.
Collins, J. H., ,,
Cornwall Library, The
Coulson, James W., *Penzance*.
Courtney, W. P., *H.M. Customs, London*.
Crotch, W. D., *Richmond*.
Cumming, Mrs., *Exmouth*.
Dale, William, *Helston*.
Davey, R., *Bochym*.
Davey, S.,　　,,
Davys, H., *Penzance*.
Dix, Rev. E.
Dix, W. G., *Truro*.
Dixon, Rev. A.
Dobell, Robert, *Royal Hotel, Truro*.
Du Boulay, Rev. H. H.
Edmonds, George, *Stamford*.
Edmonds, O.,　　　　,,
Edwards, G., *Mullyon*.
Evans, J. Bowle, *Hereford*.
Fussell, Rev. J. G. C. .. .. 2 *copies*.
Gard, W., *Breage*.
Gee, Miss E.
George, Henry, *Mullyon*.
George, John　　,,
Gilbert, Richard, ,,
Gill, John, *Truro*.
Guy, Dr., *Forest School, Walthamstow*.
Gregory, F. W., *St. Austell* .. 2 *copies*.
Grewcock, I. B., *Pershore*.
Hardy, Rev. H. H. .. .. 4 *copies*.
Hart, T., *Lizard*.
Harvey, Rev. C. F. .. 4 *copies*.
Harvey, Miss F. F.
Hawkins, Rev. E. C., *S. John's School, Leatherhead*.
Head, Mrs., *Namplough*.
Henderson, J., *Truro*.
Hendy, James, *Saltash*.

Hill, F. V., *Helston*.
Hockin, Rev. F. .. .. .. 4 *copies*.
Hockin, George.
Hockin, Miss
Hodge, Thomas, *S. Andrews, N.B.*
Hodge, T. H., *Truro*.
Howitt, G. A., ,,
Izant, John, *Frome*.
Jackson, Rev. F. C.
Jones, Rev. J. Balmer.
Joyce, J., *S. Keverne*.
Kains, Major.
Kempthorne, J. B., *S. Martyn*.
King, T., *H.M. Inspector of Schools*.
Lambe, Frederick, *London*.
Lambe, Miss A.　　,,
Leach, J., *Eastbourne*.
Le Grice, D. P. E., *Trereiffe*.
Leverton, H., *Truro*.
Leverton, Miss, *Falmouth*.
Liddicoat, H.,　　,,
Logan, C. B., *Liverpool* ... 2 *copies*.
Lowndes, Rev. M.
Lukies, R., *Mullyon*.
Lyle, Miss, *Bonython*.
MacLean, Sir John.
MacGregor, Rev. W., *Tamworth*.
Magor, Martin, *Penzance*.
Marrack, Richard, *Truro* .. 2 *copies*.
Marshall, Frederick ,, .. 2 *copies*.
Matthews, W. D. & Sons, *Lloyds' Agents, Penzance* .. .. .. 2 *copies*.
Maxwell, J., *Penzance*.
Michell, E. B.
Mitchell, W., *Western Hotel, Penzance*.
Monckton, Mrs. J. E., *Stafford*.
Munday, E., *Mullyon*.
Mundy, Miss Mary, *The "Old" Inn, Mullyon* .. .. 2 *copies*.
Mundy, M., *Mullyon*.
Mundy, Samuel, *Mullyon*.
Murray, Capt. Elibank, *R.N.*
Murray, Rev. J. W.
Nicholls, T., *Bridgenorth* .. 2 *copies*.
Nix, A. P., *Truro*.
Norris, Thomas, *Frome*.
Nunn, J. H., *A.R.A., Penzance*.

Olver, T. R., *Falmouth.*
Palmer, G. H., *London.*
Parkyn, Major, *Truro.*
Pascoe, Mrs., *St. Columb.*
Paull, Alexander, *Truro.*
Paull, John, ,,
Pearce, Horace, F.G.S., *Stourbridge.*
Pearce, Noel, *Stourbridge.*
Penberthy, Frederick, *Helston.*
Pentreath, R., *H.M. Customs, London.*
Penzance Library, The
Phillpotts, Rev. Thomas, *Porthgwidden.*
Plomer, J. G., *Helston.*
Polsue, J., *Bodmin.*
Powning, Rev. James, *Totnes.*
Pridmore, Rev. E. ... *2 copies.*
Rathbone, Mrs., *Richmond.*
Reynolds, W. J. .. .. .. *4 copies.*
Robertson, Capt. D., R.N.
Robinson, Rev. P. Vyvyan.
Rodd, E. H., *Penzance.*
Rogers, Rev. C. F.
Rogers, J., *Breage.*
Rogers, J. Jope, *Penrose.*
Rogers, R., *Carwinion.*
Rogers, Rev. Saltren.
Rogers, Rev. W. .. .. .. *2 copies.*
Romilly, G. T., *Beckenham.*
Rossiter, J. J., *S. Ives, Hunts.*
Rossiter, Thomas M , *Mells.*
Rowe, J., *Helston.*
Seccombe, Mrs., *Mullyon.*
Serres, George C., *Penzance.*
Sharp, E., *Truro.*
Shepherd, John, *Mullyon.*
Shepherd, Thomas, ,,
Skurray, S. J. C., *Great Elm, Frome.*

Solomon, Thomas, *Truro.*
Stokes, H. S., *Bodmin.*
Suffolk, W. T., *London.*
Taylor, John, ,,
Thomas, Frederick, *Mullyon.*
Thomas, John, ,,
Thomas, Jos. ,,
Thomas, Jos., *S Michael s Mount.*
Thomas, Peter, *Mullyon.*
Thomas, Thos., ,,
Thorne, J. A., *Penzance.*
Tonkin, Rev. John.. .. .. *2 copies.*
Trist, Major .. .. *2 copies.*
Tyacke, Rev. J. Sydney .. .. *5 copies.*
Tyacke, J. Walker, *Helston* .. *2 copies.*
Tyacke, Rev. R. F.
Ward, Allan O., *London* .. .. *12 copies.*
Ward, Mrs., *Eastbourne.*
Wearne, Walter, *Helston*.. .. *2 copies.*
Webb, F. H., *Wimbledon.*
Webber, Rev. F. .
Whitford, E., *St. Columb.*
Willey, John, *Mullyon.*
Willey, Thomas, *Mullyon.*
Williams, C. Hussey, *Truro.*
Williams, Dionysius, *Mullyon.*
Williams, Mrs. E., *King's Arms, Mullyon.*
Williams, George, *Scorrier* .. *2 copies.*
Williams, J., *Plymouth.*
Williams, John Michael, *Caerhays Castle.*
Williams, Michael, *Tregullow.*
Williams, Peter, *Mullyon.*
Williams, Rev. T. L.
Willyams, A. C., *Bodrean* .. *2 copies.*
Woodhouse, Rev. F. C.
Woollcombe, Rev. G. L.
Wright, Rev. F. H. A.